"*Dead Girls* is everything I want in an essay collection: provocative lines of inquiry, macabre humor, blistering intelligence. Bolin deftly lays our TV habits and pleasure reading and musical tastes in front of us, daring us to look closer. I love this book. I want to take it into the middle of a crowded room and hold it up and scream until someone tackles me to the ground; even then, I'd probably keep screaming."

—Carmen Maria Machado, author of
Her Body and Other Parties

"Bracing and blazingly smart, Alice Bolin's *Dead Girls* could hardly be more needed or more timely. A critical contribution to the cultural discussion of gender and genre, Los Angeles and noir, the unbearable persistence of the male gaze and the furtive potency of female rage."

—Megan Abbott, Edgar Award–winning
author of *You Will Know Me*

"I loved this book with reckless abandon. Alice Bolin tracks our societal fixation with violence against young women through an astonishing variety of cultural landscapes. She's a cultural critic, a grown-up girl, and, often, an enthusiastic fan of the narratives she's pulling apart, and her ability to move seamlessly between these perspectives makes for an irresistible read. It's wise and wonderful and I plan to press it on everyone I know."

—Robin Wasserman, author of *Girls on Fire*

"[An] engrossing debut collection of essays. . . . The author's voice is eerily enthralling, systematically on point, and quite funny. . . . An illuminating study on the role women play in the media and in their own lives."

—*Kirkus Reviews* (starred review)

"In her searing new essay collection, Bolin probes the generations-old obsession with young, tragic heroines. . . . Smart, thorough, and urgent, Bolin's essays are a force to be reckoned with." —*Booklist*

"A smart, incisive book about true crime and crime fiction tropes, loneliness, Los Angeles, and literature. I will be thinking about this collection for a long while."
—Sarah Weinman, author of *The Real Lolita*

"I loved reading *Dead Girls*. I knew that I was already dead, in a way, and I knew that so many of my friends and the people I saw on TV were buried here with me, but until Alice Bolin illuminated the corners of this cemetery, I didn't see the dazzling light around us. Her potent voice and nimble intertwining of the personal and the cultural form an incantation strong enough for a resurrection."
—Elissa Washuta, author of *Starvation Mode*

"With this book, Alice Bolin has singlehandedly rekindled my affection for criticism-as-memoir, offering a wry, supremely intelligent reinvention of the genre. *Dead Girls* is about living in, and through, culture; about the inseparability of art and life; about the lies we tell ourselves and other people, and the lies we love to be told. And it's just so, so funny and sad and big-hearted. I love this writer's every word and I look forward to reading her for the rest of my life."
—J. Robert Lennon, author of *Broken River*

"My copy of Alice Bolin's *Dead Girls* is a thick flutter of dog-eared pages and underlined sentences. It made me think about what I've read, and what I've written, and what I've experienced in a fresh and challenging way."
—Emily Winslow, author of *Jane Doe January*

dead girls

dead
girls

essays on surviving an american obsession

alice bolin

WILLIAM MORROW
An Imprint of HarperCollinsPublishers

FIRST EDITION

Designed by Diahann Sturge

Library of Congress Cataloging-in-Publication Data has been applied for.

ISBN 978-0-06-265714-5

18 19 20 21 22   LSC   10 9 8 7 6 5 4 3 2 1

Contents

Introduction: Girls, Girls, Girls

1.

This is a book about books. To try that again, it is a book about my fatal flaw: that I insist on learning everything from books. I find myself wanting to apologize for my book's title, which, in addition to embarrassingly taking part in a ubiquitous publishing trend by including the word *girls*, seems to evince a lurid and cutesy complicity in the very brutality it critiques. If I can say one lame thing in my defense, it is that I wanted to call this book *Dead Girls* from the moment I realized I was writing it, in the spring of 2014. I wrote an essay on the finale of the first season of *True Detective*, trying to parse a category of TV I identified as the Dead Girl Show, with *Twin Peaks* as this genre's first and still most notable example. People seemed to like that essay, so I understood that Dead Girls were something I could hitch my wagon to.

I'd moved to Los Angeles the previous summer, and I had been writing essays about that experience, too, because it was the only interesting thing I had ever done. All of the Los Angeles essays in the second section of this book were written in my first year there, as I was still learning about the city and my place in it. A lot of what I was trying to reconcile in writing about Los Angeles was my incredibly un-glamorous life there and the airbrushed city as immortalized in movies, books, and reality TV shows. When I decided to move to California, I read Raymond Chandler and Joan Didion, believing completely in their vision of Los Angeles as a sprawling, neon-lit frontier town, populated by New West prospectors trying to strike it rich in the entertainment in-dustry, haunted daily by the threat of various natural disasters.

My first night in the city, I stayed in a cheap motel off Hollywood Boulevard that I later realized I had read about in a book: the Hollywood Downtowner, prominently featured in Karolina Waclawiak's novel *How to Get into the Twin Palms*. The overlap between my reading and my life in Los Angeles stopped there. I lived in Koreatown, whose culture Chandler and Didion do not account for at all. I rode the bus, worked in food service, and had no money or friends. When I look back on this period, the vision of L.A. I bought into so unquestioningly was incredibly white and male, regardless of the fact that it was advanced by Joan Didion. It is a point of view that flattens a city of diverse neighborhoods and en-claves to a hectic series of real estate developments conceived of and controlled by a few powerful men.

Believing what I read more than my own eyes was only part of my problem, since I also did not read the right things. Take, for instance, this passage I quoted from Didion's essay

"Pacific Distances," which describes the seductive sameness of L.A. neighborhoods: "In Culver City as in Echo Park as in East Los Angeles, there are the same pastel bungalows. There are the same leggy poinsettia and the same trees of pink and yellow hibiscus." This is wrong literally and in what it implies figuratively: I saw how the crowded apartment houses of Koreatown cede abruptly to the 1920s mansions of Larchmont Village and Hancock Park. I had done the disorienting drive down Washington where the poverty of West Adams drops off at the border of Culver City. I understand where Didion was coming from: most places in L.A. are ruled by the same middle-class tract-house sensibility. As James Baldwin wrote about South Central Los Angeles in *No Name in the Street*, "Watts looks, at first, like a fine place to raise a child." But he does not lose sight of the fact that "the drive from Beverly Hills to Watts and back again is a long and loaded drive." Barbara Grizzuti Harrison, in her 1980 Didion takedown "Joan Didion: Only Disconnect," takes issue with a similar sentiment expressed in Didion's novel *The Book of Common Prayer*, where the narrator claims that poverty in the fictional Central American country of Boca Grande is "indistinguishable from comfort. We all live in cinderblock houses." "The eye that sees no difference between the cinderblock houses of the poor and the cinderblock houses of the rich is a cold, voracious one," Grizzuti Harrison writes, "it is, furthermore, astigmatic."

This voraciousness is encouraged when you are regarding the bungalows of Echo Park and East L.A. only from the windows of your car. I did not seek out work that described life in neighborhoods that weren't Hollywood or Beverly Hills, and I should have, like Paul Beatty's 1996 novel *The White Boy Shuffle*, a hilarious and damning fantasia of black life in West L.A., as feverish as *The Day of the Locust*, but with the Rodney King riots instead of zombie-fied Okies. It is a fabulist romp, like when its hero, Gunnar Kaufman, is beaten up by a teenage street gang while "playing Thoreau in the Montgomery Ward department store over in the La Cienega Mall, turning its desolate sporting goods department into a makeshift Walden"—until it isn't. Later in the same chapter, Gunnar pictures "Rodney King staggering in the Foothill Freeway's breakdown lane like a black Frankenstein, two Taser wires running 50,000 volts of electric democracy through his body."

I am especially moved by another literary account of early nineties L.A., Khadijah Queen's lyric memoir *I'm So Fine*. Queen describes it as "a list of famous men & what I had on," and it is a series of vignettes about encounters with celebrities that evolves into a meditation on womanhood and desire. When Queen writes about meeting the actor Marcus Chong as a teenager on the 105 bus, riding home from her job at Fatburger and still wearing her "ugly food service shoes," I relate deep in my heart. Most of the pieces revolve around L.A. landmarks like the Beverly Center and Universal Studios, but it feels like an artifact of Los Angeles especially because banal stories about seeing celebrities are a mainstay of L.A. discourse: for instance, the time I waited on Michael Keaton and he asked me to take away his bread.

In these stories that spin like a conversation, Queen finds

a way of telling you everything you need to know. The celebrities she is excited to encounter—Cuba Gooding Jr., DeVante Swing from Jodeci, LL Cool J—tell you what a black teenager in the early nineties was watching and listening to. The amazing outfits she describes—"my white Guess T-shirt with the gold letters tucked into high-waisted ankle-zipped acid washed jeans"—tell you what, if she was as cool as Queen, that teenager would be wearing.

But Queen also tells you much more than that. She writes despairingly at the end of one story, "why couldn't all this only be about name-dropping & brand names & pudding-tang." Despite the sensual delights she's describing, we notice the famous men beginning to take liberties from Queen's earliest experience with them. On the first page, Marcus Chong asks her to go to his house for dinner when she is eighteen, then gets angry when she says no. There are stories of comedians staring at her ass at the grocery store and rappers calling her a stuck-up bitch. She quotes Donald Trump on the privileges of celebrity, but makes a correction: "when you're a star they let you do it & actually when you're a man in general." That's why it's particularly painful when she writes about meeting Chris Tucker while working in retail: "the way he was looking at me like I was a plate of chicken & got too close & asked if I had a boyfriend which I did actually that boyfriend would rape me later that week."

As the stories in the book pile up, it becomes about the fundamental exhaustion of constantly negotiating male feelings. At the same time, Queen describes her contradictory desire for attention, especially from men who are considered important. The meditations on fashion in *I'm So Fine* express confusion about why women continue to play the game, working so hard to make ourselves acceptable to men. Despite all evidence that it's a rigged system, we believe the promises that our efforts may lead to love, fulfilled desire, and self-actualization, which I fear may explain why I would call my book, of all things, *Dead Girls*.

2.

In the winter of 2015, I was in San Bernardino, California, for a doctor's appointment when, four miles down the same street, a married couple massacred fourteen people at a holiday party for the San Bernardino County Department of Public Health. I found myself, not for the first time, compulsively refreshing a newspaper's story on the shooting, not knowing what information I was looking for. I guess I was trying to divine something about proximity, tragedy, and how random these random shootings really were, since they seemed to happen incredibly regularly in the twenty-first-century United States.

Earlier that year, my former classmate at Moscow High School in Moscow, Idaho, went on a rampage where he shot his mother, his landlord, and the manager at an Arby's before leading the police on a twenty-two-mile chase. I sought out everything I could find on the shooting, reading terse, repetitive articles from local newspapers and TV news affiliates. Especially because my classmate had changed his first and last names to John Lee, I was desperate to figure out if he was the gunman or not, hoping illogically that it was somehow another member of his family. When I saw his mug shot, I knew, but I didn't stop poring over the local news to find out what happened, looking for answers that, when they came, were predictable and sad. Reading about the case did not protect me, and it didn't instruct me either.

Moscow is a town of 25,000 people, but it experienced two mass shootings in ten years. In May 2007, Jason Hamilton murdered his wife, Crystal, and then, taking up a sniper position in the bell tower of the Presbyterian church, fired 125 bullets at the county courthouse, killing a police officer and two bystanders before committing suicide. There are details in common in the two Moscow shootings, but they're details that are common to many mass shootings. For instance, both men had stored up arsenals of weapons. When Lee was finally caught by police, he had five guns with him. A year before the shooting, Hamilton was convicted of domestic battery for strangling his girlfriend, and the court ordered him to turn in his many guns and to have a psychological examination, but he did neither. In a two-part series on the shooting, *Boise Weekly* reported that Judge John Stegner (who presided over Lee's case, too, and who is, coincidentally, the father of another of my high school classmates) "orders people to relinquish their guns nearly every day," but these orders are not regularly enforced.

The other familiar story these two cases share is the lack

of needed mental health intervention. Lee most likely suffers from paranoid schizophrenia, and he said at his sentencing, "I had amassed some guns because I felt like people were watching me, and I thought maybe my parents were trying to poison me." A police officer who was a friend of Lee's family had taken him to the hospital less than a year before his rampage because he was hearing voices, but the physician chose not to refer him for long-term psychiatric care. Hamilton had been on and off antipsychotic drugs and was committed to a mental hospital a few months before his shooting when he told a doctor "that if he were going to kill himself, he would take a bunch of people with him." (Coincidentally, this took place at the hospital where I was born, and the doctor was the doctor who delivered me.) An anonymous friend of Hamilton's wrote on an Internet message board that the real issue in the case was that Hamilton did not get the mental help he needed, saying that Crystal Hamilton "would be furious that the focus is on domestic violence and not the failings of the psych community." This ignores the fact that Hamilton's mental illness and his many domestic-violence convictions may have gone hand in hand.

There is a cliché in true crime TV that "the husband did it," and viewers yawn their way through episodes where men murder their wives for insurance money and then call 911, sobbing. It turns out the husband did it in cases of mass murder, too: according to a statistic cited in *The New York Times*, in 56 percent of mass shootings from 2009 to 2015, a spouse, former spouse, or other family member were among the victims. Domestic violence is one of the strongest indica-

tors of future mass violence, and their dynamics of control
are so similar that some experts call it "intimate terrorism."
Our refusal to address warning signs that are so common
they have become cliché means that we are not failing to prevent violence but choosing not to. Hamilton's case seems like
a baffling collective refusal to see what he was capable of.
Three months before the shooting, he told the doctor that he
planned to use a bomb or shoot people. Six days before, he
told his tattoo artist that he was going to shoot people out of
the bell tower, but the tattoo artist said, "I thought nothing
of it because he jokes about crazy-ass shit." Judge Stegner
said that he "seemed like the all-American young man," and
even though they set up a mental health court in the county
after the shooting, he worried that Hamilton would not have
been diverted to it. At some point, we choose to believe our
idea of "the all-American young man" over flags as red as
blood.

One commonality of domestic abusers and mass killers is
a sense of grievance, "a belief that someone, somewhere, had
wronged them in a way that merited a violent response," as
Amanda Taub wrote in *The New York Times* after the Pulse
nightclub shooting. Violent men's grievances are born out of
a conviction of their personal righteousness and innocence:
they are never the instigators; they are only righting what
has been done to them. This shit-eating innocence is crucial
to the fantasy of American masculinity, a bizarre collection
of expectations and tropes "so paralytically infantile," as
James Baldwin writes in "Freaks and the American Ideal of
Manhood," "that it is virtually forbidden—as an unpatriotic

act—that the American boy evolve into the complexity of manhood."

American boys have trampled most of our popular stories. In his 1949 essay "A Question of Innocence," Baldwin writes a scathing assessment of the noir, where the woman "is the incarnation of sexual evil" but "the man, . . . for all his tommy-guns and rhetoric, is the innocent, inexplicably, compulsively and perpetually betrayed." The truest love of any noir protagonist is of course never the femme fatale, for "the boy cannot know a woman since he has never become a man." American boys in their grievance and longing invented their dream girl, the Dead Girl. My interest in the boy heroes of *Twin Peaks* and Raymond Chandler spawned the first essays for this book, which began as an exploration of the noir mysteries of the American West and ended up as something more like a survival guide, as the violence I studied hit ever closer to me. Like other writers before me, I have tried to make something about women from stories that were always and only about men.

Part 1

The Dead Girl Show

Toward a Theory of a
Dead Girl Show

*T*win Peaks, David Lynch's early nineties noir fantasy
about small-town Washington, provides thirty of the
oddest and most influential hours in the history of television. I
watched them all in my little apartment in Missoula, Montana, with stolen Internet, twenty years late. I was prepared
for it to be a relentlessly quirky murder mystery, with its
sweet and idiosyncratic hero, FBI agent Dale Cooper; the
bizarre Twin Peaks townies, like the woman who carries
around a psychically gifted log; the story's flirtation with the
supernatural, including visions, demons, and aliens; and
the town's supremely seductive teenage girls, whose saddle
shoes and sweater sets say, "Welcome to Twin Peaks. Please
set your clocks back forty years."

I wasn't prepared for how, in its stubborn weirdness, it
tells a story at least as old as America. As Greil Marcus outlines in his essay "Picturing America," *Twin Peaks* is manifest
from the film noir tradition, a genre that is obsessed with

setting. The mid-century detective stories of Raymond Chandler and Ross Macdonald are less about the criminal mind than systemic corruption: cities that are growing too fast, both booming from the war and reeling from its losses. "It was the pretentious, provincial city . . . ," Marcus says of the "Film Noir City," "where the most respectable citizen is always the most criminal, a town big enough to get murders written up as suicides and small enough that no one outside the place cares what happens there."

Lynch's innovation to the form was to add something more psychologically elemental. *Twin Peaks*'s plot is sparked by the murdered body of seventeen-year-old Laura Palmer, washed up on the bank of a river. Palmer's corpse is *Twin Peaks*'s truly memorable image: river-wet hair slicked around her perfect porcelain face, blue with death but still tranquil, lovely. One question, "Who killed Laura Palmer?," spawned a genre—*Veronica Mars*, *The Killing*, *Pretty Little Liars*, *Top of the Lake*, *True Detective*, *How to Get Away with Murder*, and *The Night Of* are notable descendants of *Twin Peaks*. All Dead Girl Shows begin with the discovery of the murdered body of a young woman. The lead characters of the series are attempting to solve the (often impossibly complicated) mystery of who killed her. As such, the Dead Girl is not a "character" in the show, but rather, the memory of her is.

The first season of *True Detective* follows two Louisiana detectives, Rust Cohle and Marty Hart, as they attempt to solve a series of bizarre murders. The show opens in 1995, with Hart and Cohle inspecting a prostitute's corpse that has been posed and bound to a tree in a clearing in the Louisiana wilderness, a crown of deer antlers affixed to her head. The season proceeds along two parallel tracks, as Hart and Cohle search for the murderer in 1995, and as they recall the events of their 1995 investigation seventeen years later, in 2012. *True Detective* generated the kind of cult hysteria that only a Dead Girl can. On the night of the season finale, fans crashed HBO's Internet streaming service with their "overwhelming popular demand" for the series. I watched it in my bedroom in Los Angeles, attempting to have something to talk about with my coworkers. Instead I ended up making sarcastic notes about the show on my phone, simultaneously annoyed and inspired by the almost sublime heavy-handedness of its entire mission.

The cinematography in the first season is moody, elegant, and gorgeous. Its A-list lead actors, Matthew McConaughey and Woody Harrelson, give swaggering, juicy performances. Legendary alt-country producer T Bone Burnett provided the soundtrack, another of *True Detective*'s gestures toward being classy, southern Gothic, literary. This is a brilliant ruse: a generic specimen of cultural camp pretending to appeal to its audience *intellectually*. The characters have the monosyllabic bastard-Dickensian names found in every airport paperback: Rust Cohle? Episode four takes a weird turn into another region of thrillerville, as Cohle infiltrates a motorcycle gang he was associated with in his former undercover work and instigates a drug-related shootout in a housing project. Cohle is haunted by the memory of his dead daughter—have you heard that one before? Perhaps in every popular portrayal of a detective ever?

I think *True Detective* mania mostly owes itself to the complicated power of the Dead Girl Show. The Dead Girl Show's notable themes are its two odd, contradictory messages for women. The first is that girls are wild, vulnerable creatures who need to be protected from the power of their own sexualities. *True Detective* demonstrates a self-conscious, conflicted fixation on strippers and sex workers. Hart helps "free" a teenage prostitute from a brothel and, seven years later, cheats on his wife with her. "How does she even know about that stuff?" Hart asks in 1995 when he and his wife discover sexual drawings his elementary-school-age daughter made. "Girls always know first," his wife replies. This terrible feminine knowledge has been a trope at least since Eve in the Garden. Marcus compares *Twin Peaks*'s victim Laura Palmer to the teenage "witches" in Puritan New England who were targeted to purge and purify their communities. In the Dead Girl Show, the girl body is both a wellspring of and a target for sexual wickedness.

The other message the Dead Girl Show has for women is simpler: trust no dad. Father figures and male authorities hold a sinister interest in controlling girl bodies, and therefore in harming them. In *True Detective*, the conspiracy goes all the way to the top, involving politicians and clergymen. In *Twin Peaks*, Palmer's father is her murderer—sort of. It turns out that he is possessed by a demon named Bob, who has driven him to rape Laura for years. Sheriff Truman expresses his disbelief in the demon story. "Harry," says Agent Cooper, "is it easier to believe that a man could rape and murder his own daughter?" As if this is something that has never happened before—that doesn't, in fact, happen all the time. As if a large majority of sexual assaults (73 percent) are not committed by someone the victim knows, and a significant percentage (7 percent) are not committed by family members.

Externalizing the impulse to prey on young women cleverly depicts it as both inevitable and beyond the control of men. Marcus's essay is a meditation on how the Dead Girl Show reflects and appeals to the American psyche, which is imprinted with the memory of two inherited atrocities, slavery and the genocide of American Indians. He discusses the resonance of old murder ballads that tell us that "America is a country where anyone can be killed at any time, for any reason, or no reason at all." Murder is something on the air, like a demon—and make no mistake, this is a kind of victim blaming.

True Detective crucially involves history, too. In the first episode, Cohle tells Hart almost admiringly that the murder shows "vision." "Vision has meaning," he says, "and meaning is historical." The show's ritualistic murders invoke voodoo and southern Louisiana's unique brand of Catholicism. Leading into the finale, Errol Childress, the horrifying inbred Faulknerian psychopath who is the villain of the show, the self-styled Yellow King, says menacingly into the camera, "My family's been here a long, long time." But the show is also rooted in a landscape of indeterminacy where history can be destroyed and effaced. They talk about the lawlessness after Hurricane Katrina, hospitals and churches and people that have been lost along the disappearing coastline.

Broadening the effect and the meaning of an individual

murder is what the Dead Girl Show is all about. Investigating these murders essentially ruins Cohle's and Hart's lives. When we see them in 2012, Cohle is gaunt and bedraggled, now a bartender who starts drinking at noon on his day off. Hart is off the force, too, and divorced, drinking again and working as a private eye. How sad that these murders had to happen *to them*. The show's trademark is Cohle's laughably *serious* dialogue about the nature of the self and existence. He describes life as "a dream that you had inside a locked room. A dream about being a person." These ruminations recall Plato's Cave, in which the self is a prison that prevents true insight. In *Twin Peaks*, Detective Cooper visits a mysterious red room in his dreams where he has grotesque visions and receives urgent spiritual messages. It is his labyrinthine consciousness made manifest, just as in the last episode of *True Detective*, Cohle and Hart enter Childress's lair, Carcosa, a creepy series of buildings, ramparts, and underground passages, confronting the heart of their own darkness.

Cohle even hallucinates a swirling funnel cloud in the sky before coming face-to-face with Childress, hitting home that this is a journey into his own mind. "There's just one story, the oldest," Cohle tells Hart at the end of the finale, "light versus dark." He has come to a breakthrough, a new understanding, some small peace. As Marcus wrote about *Twin Peaks*, "the story will be over before it begins." There can be no redemption for the Dead Girl, but it is available to the person who is solving her murder. Just as for the murderers, for the detectives in *True Detective* and *Twin Peaks*, the victim's body is a neutral arena on which to work out male problems.

Pretty Little Liars was an ABC Family show with a giant fan base among teenage girls. It centers on four high schoolers—Spencer Hastings, Aria Montgomery, Emily Fields, and Hanna Marin—as they attempt to solve the murder of their friend and queen bitch, Alison DiLaurentis. A year after Alison's disappearance, the girls start to receive threatening texts from a mysterious psychopath called only A. A is ubiquitous and all-powerful. Over the course of the series, A has filmed the girls, photographed them, listened to their conversations, read their emails, stolen from them, revealed their secrets, locked them in basements and closets, faked Spencer's boyfriend's death, and hit Hanna with a car, to give only a very short list. I watched the first two seasons breathlessly at my friend Emily's house in Missoula, and for a while I would jump in fear whenever I got a text message.

A's outrageousness is indicative of *Pretty Little Liars*'s guiding ethic. The show manically collects characters, story lines, mysteries, and red herrings, so that its plot becomes a baffling web of unanswered questions. Since Alison's disappearance, there have been many more murders, few of which have been satisfyingly solved. More than a hundred episodes later, we grow only incrementally closer to an answer to the initial mystery. One can assume that the show's creators are, to some extent, fucking with their audience, but I admire the audacity with which they have dodged and complicated every moment of resolution.

With its bizarrely powerful villain and its bizarrely complicated plot, *Pretty Little Liars* evokes nothing so much as a fairy tale. Marcus discusses the importance of *Twin Peaks*'s mysterious forest setting, and a forest figures importantly in *Pretty Little Liars*, too. The show's lead characters meet in the forest, are chased in it, pursue a girl in a fairy tale's red-hooded coat who looks so much like Alison through it—is she dead or isn't she? The woods are shadowy, uncertain places, sympathetic to secrets, magic, transformations, and cruelty. Fairy tales are weird, distilled expressions of our inherited desires, and the Dead Girl Show, with its idyllic, uncanny small-town setting, is absolutely in the same tradition—it is no wonder that Sigmund Freud believed fairy tales could be interpreted like collective dreams.

Dead Girl Shows often experiment with the incest taboo, like the girls on *Pretty Little Liars*, *Veronica Mars*, and *Top of the Lake* who share kisses with characters they later learn could be their half brothers. This goes back to Freud's favorite myth, Oedipus, in which a prince is fated to kill his father and marry his mother, and the psychological metaphors of Gothic literature, and the imposing persistence of patriarchal authority. My bad dad is your bad dad, as if to say, is everyone's bad dad. And characters on Dead Girl Shows often experience frustrating lacunae in their memories. Laura Palmer's father doesn't remember anything he does while the demon Bob controls him. Duncan Kane, whose sister, Lilly, is the Dead Girl on *Veronica Mars*, suffers from a strange mental illness in which he has violent episodes that he doesn't remember later. Both Alison's brother and Spencer on *Pretty*

Little Liars had substance-related blackouts on the night of Alison's murder, making them question their own innocence. These memory gaps are related to Freudian repressions, evoking the fraught landscape of the unknowable self.

Maggie Nelson writes in *The Art of Cruelty* how Freud's centralizing of the Oedipus complex structures the human psyche around a question of personal guilt: "He . . . placed the questions 'What have I done?,' 'Am I a criminal?,' . . . at the heart of self-inquiry." And the story of Oedipus Rex, like Dead Girl stories, is also about family secrets and the sins of the father. As Nelson writes in *The Red Parts*,

> Conventional wisdom has it that we dredge up
> family stories to find out more about ourselves . . .
> to catapult ourselves, like Oedipus, down the
> track that leads to the revelation of some original
> crime . . . Then we gouge our eyes out in shame.

In the two great feminist Dead Girl Shows, *Veronica Mars* and *Top of the Lake*, the female protagonist is both trying to solve the mystery presented by a Dead (or missing) Girl and to solve her own rape, making the question not "What have I done?" but "What happened to me?" Nonetheless, memory and the self are presented as riddles to be solved.

But there is an alternative to this mystery-solution model of the human wound. As Nelson points out—and as is borne out by the glut of Dead Girl Shows and their incredible popularity—our most basic myth would seem to be not Oedipus's patricide, but matricide and violence against women. Where is Cinderella's mother, and where is Little Red Riding Hood's grandmother? The philosopher Julia Kristeva has explained the drive toward matricide as a kind of original, generative anger, expressing a need to destroy the mother, the origin place, to become an individual self. This is messier than an Oedipal reading of history, as the will to matricide is born in confusion and creates only chaos. As Nelson explains, the maternal element returns "via horror, repulsion, the uncanny, haunting, melancholia, depression, guilt."

The Red Parts is Nelson's personal account of the trial of the man who murdered her aunt before Nelson was born. The strangest part of Nelson's story is her family's experience participating in an episode of the true crime show *48 Hours Mystery* about the murder. Nelson becomes a character in *48 Hours*'s version, the writer niece whose work is fascinated with her aunt's death. A producer tells Nelson that their episode will help other people mourn, but, thinking of the list of titles for previous episodes—like "Where's Baby Sabrina?" and "JonBenét: DNA Rules Out Parents"—she asks him "if there's a reason why stories about the bizarre, violent deaths of young, good-looking, middle-to-upper-class white girls help people to mourn better than other stories."

Clearly Dead Girls help us work out our complicated feelings about the privileged status of white women in our culture. The paradox of the perfect victim, effacing the deaths of leagues of nonwhite or poor or ugly or disabled or immigrant or drug-addicted or gay or trans victims, encapsulates the combination of worshipful covetousness and violent rage that drives the Dead Girl Show. The white girl becomes the highest sacrifice, the virgin martyr, particularly to that most unholy idol of narrative. As Nelson writes, all the jumbled details of her aunt's murder that she had stewed over, "years of compulsion, confusion, and damage," became a satisfying story under *48 Hours*'s gaze, and "not just any story—a 'story of struggle and hope.'" But to achieve that seductive conclusion, the story must be over before it begins. Nelson writes how in college she watched Alfred Hitchcock's film *Vertigo* in a class on existentialism, and she was disturbed "by the way Kim Novak's character seems stranded between ghost and flesh, whereas Jimmy Stewart seems 'real.'" She had the impulse to ask her professor "whether women were somehow always already dead, or, conversely, had somehow not yet begun to exist."

Inasmuch as *Pretty Little Liars* is a Dead Girl Show taken to its logical extreme, the trespasses, sexual and otherwise, of its male authorities are too numerous to name: there are untrustworthy fathers, teachers, doctors, and police officers. It is also notable among other Dead Girl Shows in its absence of a strong protagonist or pair of protagonists, heroes on a quest. All Dead Girl Shows betray an Oedipal distrust of male authority figures, but in *Twin Peaks* and *True Detective*, the central characters *are* male authority figures. These shows glide to a single, comprehensive solution, reflecting the Freudian model of existence that, according to Nelson, "turns our lives into detective stories; our innermost selves, into culprits." At every moment, *Pretty Little Liars* refuses the unified answer—with its four protagonists, with its many villains and many victims, with the way it multiplies with mysteries, with its Dead Girl who refuses to stay dead.

Since the first text from the ambiguously named A, the main question of *Pretty Little Liars* has been not who killed Alison, but whether she is dead at all. In her friends' memories of her, she is terrifying and manipulative; a major theme in the series is how she controls them even after death with the secrets she knew. In earlier seasons, the girls often have vivid, enigmatic visions of her. As all we have repressed returns, so this Dead Girl persistently becomes a presence in a story that was supposed to be about her absence. What would seem to be *Pretty Little Liars*'s worst faults—its unwieldy plot, its lack of consistency, the culpability of so many characters—are actually instructive. Its creators have made a Dead Girl Show that is not about a journey toward existential knowledge instigated by a Dead Girl body, but the mess, the calamity, and the obscurity that are the consequences of misogyny.

Black Hole

I was born in the late eighties in Moscow, Idaho, a small university town in a region of undulating loess hills called the Palouse. Just past the University of Idaho campus, fields jut up in steep dunes, a unique Ice Age geological feature appearing all the more alien when combine harvesters drag the fertile hillsides at a forty-five-degree angle to the highway. The house I grew up in in Moscow was a green-engineering experiment: an agricultural engineer at the University of Idaho built it in 1948 out of lightweight concrete made from sawdust and diatomaceous earth. This was apparently so pioneering that the house was on the cover of *Mother Earth News* thirty years later.

As you might imagine, it did not look like a normal house. It was a giant rectangle set into a slope, so you entered on the second floor. This was by design: the bedrooms stayed cool in the summer and warm in the winter, partially insulated underground. My parents painted it peach with orange trim, and then, on an angry whim, my dad painted the house numbers three feet tall in orange on the chimney, so pizza drivers would stop passing it by mistake. Inside, the walls curved instead of forming angles, and the decor was stuck in its *Mother Earth News* glory days. In our living room, there was an ocean-colored shag carpet and a built-in couch upholstered in swirling, psychedelic greens and blues. The kitchen table was an amoeba-shaped slab attached to a glittery diner booth.

The Technicolor quirk of the house was juxtaposed with our huge, overgrown yards. It was built on two lots, with descending terraces in the front yard and stands of pines in back. The yards had bushes, lilac trees, a raspberry bramble, and various little gardens my dad planted. This was the setting for my feral and morbid childhood pretends, where it was easy to imagine that I was a tragic runaway setting up house in the shelter of a giant fir. My little brother and I would prance around the yard in a pair of ruffly ballet tutus like a couple of forest sprites. I know it sounds like a fairy tale, and as is true in fairy tales, my sawdust palace was an idyll edged in peril. My neighborhood climbed up in massive, steep hills on all sides of my house. I would gawk—infuriatingly, I'm sure—at my dad as he slowly pushed his bike up the hill. The wild neighbor kids rode their dirt bikes through our backyard and sped down the hills with their butts on their skateboards directly into heavy traffic.

Growing up with such bizarre splendor and danger implanted in me a kind of comfort with the sublime that can't have been healthy. Everyone knows the American West embodies the twin ideals of beauty and terror—the intersection of the awful and the awesome—but growing up in a homely little town set against a lush and extreme landscape is freakier than that. Moscow is an obscure eighty-mile drive from the interstate. The Palouse is the middle of nowhere: a nowhere with quilted hills of wheat and soybeans stacking and cresting like the waves of the ocean. *No one is watching*, the uncanny countryside seems to say. *Anything is possible.*

The idea that northwestern landscapes hide some sinister, almost literary meaning was underscored by the news stories of my childhood, when serial killers and neo-Nazis brought my region to the pages of national newspapers. Ruby Ridge and the Unabomber's cabin—one a few hours north of Moscow, the other half a day's drive west in Lincoln, Montana—sent a clear message: the Inland Northwest makes people go nuts, or, less superstitiously, it is where white men with chips on their shoulders feel they belong. The siege at Ruby Ridge occurred in 1992, a time when I wasn't exactly reading the newspaper, and confusion about it threaded through my childhood. But I knew even then that its narratives hung on the remoteness and majesty of where the disaster occurred: the story was named after the jagged hilltop in northern Idaho where Christian separatist and fugitive Randy Weaver and his family homesteaded. After the government's attempt to apprehend Weaver ended with the deaths of a U.S. marshal and Weaver's wife and fourteen-year-old son, FBI agent Gene Glenn asked the mountains, "How could there be so much evil in such a beautiful place?" As if beauty were ever incompatible with chaos.

The Weavers were drawn to North Idaho from Iowa in

1983 by a mix of conspiracy theories and creative scriptural and literary interpretation, convinced that God was sending Vicki Weaver messages in biblical passages, Ayn Rand novels, and stories by H. G. Wells. They believed they must wait out the Great Tribulation on a lonely mountaintop, avoiding interference from the "Zionist Occupied Government." They were hardly alone in finding the Northwest the ideal place to hide and wait. Jess Walter writes in his 1995 nonfiction account, *Ruby Ridge*, that North Idaho "always attracted people whose only common trait was the overwhelming desire to just *get away*."

As Walter notes, in the sixties and seventies, many of those getting away to the Northwest were from the opposite end of the political spectrum as the Weavers: "hippies, draft dodgers, and an entire back-to-the-land movement." Nevertheless, as the stories of every species of Idaho recluse make clear, to many people, isolation seems to be the Inland Northwest's primary characteristic and its only selling point. And when right-wing separatists like the Weavers started overrunning the region in the early eighties—"a blurring continuum," as Walter describes them, "of home schoolers, Christian survivalists, apocalyptics, John Birchers, Posse Comitatus members, constitutionalists, tax protesters, Identity Christians, and Neo-Nazis"—the hills weren't going to say anything against them.

Walter started his career as a newspaper reporter for *The Spokesman-Review*, the region's only major newspaper, and he describes Ruby Ridge as his "Truman Capote moment." The paper broke the story, and he and other *Spokesman-*

Review reporters were finalists for the Pulitzer Prize for their coverage of the standoff. From there, Walter charted an unusual literary trajectory, starting with *Ruby Ridge*, then cowriting O. J. Simpson prosecutor Chris Darden's memoir and putting out a few thrillers before crossing over into respectability with a string of four acclaimed literary novels.

Throughout Walter's work, the town of Spokane, Washington, where he has lived his entire life, looms large. Spokane is an unglamorous blue-collar city with a population of 200,000 on the eastern edge of Washington, ninety-five miles away from Ruby Ridge. "A poor, isolated city," Walter says, "that peaked in the 1920s." Walter developed the inferiority complex common to many people from weird working-class towns whose ambitions stretch beyond their neighborhoods. "I wanted to be a literary novelist," he said of his early career. "And I thought, *You can't get there from where I am. You can't get there from Spokane.*"

My parents used to tell me that about North Idaho, joking that the region's motto should be "You can't get there from here." But they meant it literally. Idaho is one of the only states without a north-south interstate highway, and its only north-south route, the treacherous U.S. Route 95, was famously described in 1970 by Idaho governor Cecil Andrus as "the goat trail." My main memories of Highway 95 were eleven-hour bus trips to Pocatello with my high school choir, where I was trapped, listening to the mom chaperones talk about Weight Watchers as the bus inched its way down narrow, wooded canyons. When we were going to Boise, a comparatively breezy five-hour trip, it often made more sense to drive south by going west, making use of the interstates in Washington and Oregon. "There are no roads!" my dad would yell. You can't get there from here.

So when Walter told the literary magazine *Willow Springs*, "I think Spokane is one of the most isolated cities of its size in the United States, and that its isolation casts a lot of different shadows," the geographical fades into the emotional and back again. Its isolation gives Spokane what Walter calls a "lab quality": "as if you could have any kind of experiment here you wanted." This extends from fiction—that any kind of character or story set in Spokane could be believable—to the real-life hippie and neo-Nazi experimenters who also saw the Inland Northwest as a blank slate.

Maybe the lab quality is why northwestern true crime stories, Ruby Ridge and so many others, tend to be bizarre and bombastic. Late in 1983, long before the standoff at Ruby Ridge, a group of Aryan Nations members met in a barn in eastern Washington and swore an oath to "deliver our people from the Jew and bring total victory to the Aryan race." Calling themselves the Brüder Schweigen ("Silent Brotherhood") or simply the Order, the men waged a terrorist campaign that started with robbing a Spokane bank, escalating to bombing a Boise synagogue and killing a Jewish radio host in Denver. Along the way they robbed banks and armored cars, stealing millions of dollars. The remoteness of the region drew these antisocial figures and enabled their crime spree, as they could plan in secret and scatter into the western wilderness after the deeds were done.

Washington State was also home to several of the twentieth century's notorious serial killers, including Ted Bundy and the Green River Killer. Walter reported on four serial killers in his time at *The Spokesman-Review*. One reason for this pattern is the relative wildness of even the state's most developed areas. "It allows a killer to move from an urban area to a rural area in a fairly short period of time," criminologist Steve Egger told *The Seattle Times*. "You have pockets of wilderness, lots and lots of pockets, where bodies can be dumped, and where they would be very difficult to find." Experts are eager to insist that the prevalence of serial killers in the region is a myth, that the northwestern states rank among the lowest in murder rates. But that is not what these sensational stories broadcast to the world. And if the world perceives the Northwest as a region in the grips of extremists and psychopaths, what does that mean for everyone else who happens to be born there?

Walter's experience covering northwestern serial killers for *The Spokesman-Review* inspired his first novel, the 2001 crime thriller *Over Tumbled Graves*. As Walter explains about the book's origins, he was disturbed by the post–Hannibal Lecter temptation to make the serial killer an attractively terrifying villain, "not only dangerous and twisted, but super-intelligent, possibly even supernatural. They had to be the most interesting characters in the book and it was even better if they were people with wit and style and aplomb."

His interactions with real-life psychopaths revealed them to be anything but charming geniuses: they were instead "the kind of broken, weak-minded loser who preys on women on the fringe of society." *Over Tumbled Graves* consciously takes on the American obsession with serial killers and the industry that's sprung up around mythologizing murderers, and it stresses a truth that mystery novelists and true crime writers don't want to acknowledge: that serial killers are, "in some important and horrifying way, smaller than life." This revelation of how dumb and small evil really is makes *Over Tumbled Graves* a brutal, brilliant, and underrated novel, which should be considered among all of Walter's later, more "literary" output.

The book's serial killer is hunting Spokane's prostitutes, and his first victim is found in the city's Riverfront Park, her decomposing body described in awful detail: "her leathery skin hung in place, shrink-wrapped around the bone, flesh drying away"; her "small head, already shrinking in on itself," with "lips pulled tight around her teeth, as if she had eaten something sour." As he uncovers her, the wry and weary Detective Alan Dupree thinks ruefully to himself, subtitling the novel he has found himself in, "The things men do to women."

Dupree is sensitive and iconoclastic, upsetting his colleagues in the Spokane Police Department with his strange sense of humor and cosmic theories of criminology. At times he speaks in koans that could have inspired *True Detective*'s investigator sage, Rust Cohle: Dupree ruminates that "We're all fixed points on a circle." Of course, the figure of the philosopher detective—Dupree's colleagues call him "Officer Philosopher"—is an archetype that can be traced back to Sherlock Holmes and earlier. By initially placing a character like Dupree at the forefront of the investigation, privileging his thoughts and theories, Walter fakes his audience out. In a novel about what men do to women, no man can be completely absolved.

Dupree still falls prey to what he calls "the humiliating excitement of a murder investigation." He views crime as a natural phenomenon, like a weather pattern, which comes and goes in streaks like seasons, and the serial killer as a pure "bad guy" whose habits are too dark and powerful to be conceived of: "the criminal equivalent of a black hole." As we come to see, although this perspective is attractive in the telling of crime stories, it mystifies the killer in ways that are not only counterproductive but also insidious.

The real protagonist of *Over Tumbled Graves* is Detective Caroline Mabry, who trained with Dupree and who has conducted a long, rarely spoken of emotional love affair with him. Her unfulfilled love and the death of her mother leave Caroline set apart and set adrift, characteristics that become her greatest asset. Caroline is in a fog of grief and guilt, unable to see more than the evidence in front of her, which prevents her from forming any grand theories of the case: the mistake all of the male investigators, including Dupree, fall victim to.

The FBI profilers working with the department intellectualize the case most repulsively. They are obsessed with serial killers' MOs, finding patterns of behavior that illuminate the killers' backgrounds and psychology. As former FBI profiler Curtis Blanton tells Caroline, "With these guys, it all goes back to fantasy." He is adamant that inhabiting that fantasy, the sexual and control-based kicks killers get from killing, is how the police can understand and solve these crimes. The most disturbing thing about Blanton's belief in understanding "the fantasy" is how he frames it as something that comes naturally to male investigators, as if the monstrous desire to brutalize women lies dormant in all men—as if it's actually a power that men possess, terrible but formidable. Caroline sees that this affirmation of the killer's inner life will eventually blame the victim. The Spokane Police Department's prime suspect had a girlfriend who was murdered while working as a prostitute, which leads both profilers to an "excitation/ retaliation model": "Ultimately, both profilers wrote, Ryan blamed his girlfriend for her own death and for his killing spree. *She made him do it.*"

"I've never met a woman who contributed much to these kinds of cases," Blanton tells Caroline about female investigators. "Fortunately for them, they don't have the capacity for understanding this type of killer, for understanding the fantasy." As the book goes on, Caroline begins to question why anyone would want to. "If she couldn't imagine the fantasy, what could she imagine?" Walter writes. "The victim. The fear." This is when we begin to see that *Over Tumbled Graves* is a different kind of serial killer novel: one that is blessedly more interested in the victims' state of mind than the killer's. In the novel's climactic final scene, a victim calls out for help and Caroline "[thinks] the woman's voice might be her own."

By rejecting popular criminal myths, *Over Tumbled Graves* insists that serial killers' minds are not singular. They're a dime a dozen. When Caroline reviews her notes from interviews she's conducted with prostitutes, "words leaped from the pages: 'bit' and 'punched' and 'knifed' and 'choked' and 'bruised,' stories of gang rape at knifepoint, of violations with beer bottles and guns." She concludes that "it might be easier to eliminate the white men in pickup trucks who didn't scare these hookers." This sounds like an exaggeration, but it is eerily echoed in *The Spokesman-Review*'s July 2001 series "The Trail to a Serial Killer" about the real-life murderer Robert Yates, who killed at least thirteen women working as prostitutes in Spokane between 1996 and 1998, and who would seem to be Walter's direct inspiration for *Over Tumbled Graves*. The paper describes how "passersby pelt prostitutes with BBs, pennies, tomatoes, bottles, bleach. Johns smack them, cut them, rob them, handcuff them, gang rape them, leave them miles from town." One of the prostitutes whom Yates murdered had previously been stuffed in a sleeping bag by an angry john and thrown in the Spokane River. After investigating prostitutes' experiences, the police on the Yates case figured, astoundingly, that "there [were] several dozen men capable of committing these kinds of murders."

Walter has said that *Over Tumbled Graves* was informed by the Yates murders but wasn't based on them; it was released two weeks before Yates was even arrested. Walter maintains that he had plenty of other inspiration—including several serial killers he covered while working at *The Spokesman-Review*—saying, "It's horrifying to realize how many men have been stalking women in Spokane." This is, of course, the practical problem. As Blanton tells Caroline, "There's very good reason

I don't see many women investigators on cases like this. It's not natural." Then why is it natural for male investigators? At times in the novel, the equivalence of male officer to predator seems one-to-one. Caroline notes that her male colleagues seem to prefer unidentified victims, "far more comfortable with a body that had no connection to a living person"—just as murderers do. There is something enlightening here about our understanding of the abstraction "crime" encompassing both the process of committing a crime and the process of solving it. If these stories—of *Over Tumbled Graves*, Robert Yates, Ruby Ridge, and all the other northwestern sociopaths—have one thing in common, every step of the way, it's men. Men are the problem.

Ruby Ridge is seen as a case where extremes tragically met and combusted: the Weavers' extreme lifestyle and ideology and the U.S. government's extremes of arrogance, disorganization, and violence. So much about the standoff is still clouded in ambiguity: who shot first, what kind of force the FBI authorized, and whom the sniper who shot Vicki Weaver was aiming at. As Walter writes, "Tens of millions of dollars have been spent on hearings and investigations that failed to resolve the most basic questions about the standoff." But what seems clear is a lesson here about *escalation*: the difficulty of denying a challenge, the temptation of responding not as we are but as we, always monstrously, wish to see ourselves.

In a judgment in the ten-million-dollar civil suit Kevin Harris, Randy Weaver's friend who was injured in the standoff, lodged against the government, the Ninth Circuit Court

of Appeals condemned the FBI's actions as "a wholly un-
warranted return to a lawless and arbitrary Wild West school
of law enforcement." It may be that the agents and officials
involved in the Ruby Ridge case were seduced by its untamed
setting, envisioning themselves as the only defenders of justice on the vast, lonesome range. And Weaver was just as
susceptible to these Wild West archetypes. When news broke
that the fugitive Weaver had refused to leave his mountaintop
cabin, the family received attention from the national media
and letters of support from around the country, dangerously
inflating Randy's view of his own importance. One news
crew told the Weavers that Randy was becoming "a Wild
West hero, like his boyhood hero, Jesse James."

It's no surprise that Weaver chose to believe this version of
himself over the truth: that he was, as a report from the U.S.
marshals said, "lazy and quite possibly a coward," putting
his family in danger to protect himself. But it's also the version that the government ultimately bought into, with the FBI
warning their agents that Weaver was dangerous and highly
skilled, a former Green Beret. It's another case of destructive
masculinity requiring both one's self and one's enemy to be
larger than life. These icons of masculinity are so exaggerated
in the American West—the outlaw, the sheriff, the cowboy, the
Indian—because there was so much irony and uncertainty and
fear to outweigh in the conquest of the continent, so much cruelty and greed to conceal. It's like a scene in Sherman Alexie's
novel *Indian Killer*, when a white farmer explains that he's justified in shooting American Indians who are harvesting camas
root on his land. "This land has been in our family for over a

hundred years," he tells his son. "And those Indians are stealing from us."

Alexie's novel also illustrates how Wild West narratives seep painfully into modern life. *Indian Killer* tells the story of John Smith, an American Indian boy who is adopted by white parents in Seattle. John's identity is fraught from the beginning, as he fantasizes about his birth mother and the life he would have had with her on the reservation, not knowing which tribe's reservation to imagine. This alienation is both compounded and mirrored by John's worsening mental illness; he hears voices and often has visions of the Indian priest who baptized him. Most of the novel centers on the story of a serial killer who is preying on white men in Seattle. His melodramatic MO, scalping his victims and leaving eagle feathers as a signature, earns him the nickname Indian Killer.

The initial obvious solution to the book's mystery is that the Indian Killer is one facet of John's troubled personality. Without a native culture of his own, John's cultural expression is exaggeratedly eclectic and shallow: his apartment is "decorated with brightly lit posters of fancy dancers . . . A laguna pot, a miniature rug, a Navajo rug stapled to the wall. A gigantic dreamcatcher, which was supposed to entrap nightmares, was suspended over the bed." It is believable that John would have resorted to such a sensational and stereotypical performance—the bloodthirsty brave scalping white settlers—for his rage. John is a blank slate, the generic Indian, whose confused identity is a model for how white texts and imposed stereotypes have shaped American Indian self-image.

But others in the novel seem to view John as a blank slate, too. Jack Wilson, a white mystery novelist who claims obscure Indian ancestry, writes about Aristotle Little Hawk, "the very last Shilshomish Indian, who was a practicing medicine man and private detective in Seattle." When Wilson sees John, he is shocked at his resemblance to the Little Hawk of his imagination. It seems John can stand in for any Indian archetype, the noble savage or the savage killer. The Indian Killer could be just another hackneyed role that others would have John play. At times it seems like the Indian Killer is a true bogeyman, not an expression of Indian anger but white fear, materialized.

The Indian Killer's first victim is an arrogant college student, "his head high and shoulders wide." The Killer stalks him, filled with hatred for the man's swagger and expensive clothes. In this way, Alexie frames *Indian Killer* as simple wish fulfillment. He got the idea for the novel in college, saying, "I was sitting at Washington State with frat guys in the back row who I wanted to kill. And I would fantasize about murder." But the violence and anger that propel the novel can camouflage the complicated meta-moves it is performing, as it comments on genre and itself. Alexie draws a parallel between the stereotypes that constrain American Indian identity and the oppressive expectations of genre, which is also a matrix of received texts and traditions. Wilson is writing a novel about the Indian Killer, a strange mirror version of Alexie's own, which forces the reader to consider how the story would play out in a traditional mystery. Characters comment on the predictable trajectory of their own story.

"Besides, you know how this will go in real life," Wilson's agent tells him. "In the third act, they'll find out some white guy with eagle feathers is doing the killing. White guys are always the serial killers."

The height of parody in *Indian Killer* is the white American Indian Studies professor Dr. Mather, who was supposedly "adopted into a Lakota Sioux family." A transparent stand-in for the long line of misguided white people who have written American Indian history, Mather serves as Alexie's foil to complicate the aims of the novel. Mather says of one of the Indian Killer's crimes, "The kidnapping of Mark Jones is actually a bold, albeit cowardly, metaphor for the Indian condition. Indian people have had their culture, their children, metaphorically stolen by European colonization." Because this theory is put forth by the ridiculous Mather, it preempts the reader from coming to such a simple interpretation.

Ultimately the novel inhabits a place of painful ambiguity, as symbolized by John's undecided identity. In an interview with *The Guardian* in 2003, Alexie said *Indian Killer* was by far his least popular book because people were repulsed by its violence. But as he pointed out, it is a story of doubles and parallels, where each act of trauma receives one in return: "There was an Indian kid being kidnapped and a white kid being kidnapped. Everyone failed to see any ambiguity." There is even confusion implanted in the novel's title, a question voiced by a character that seems obvious once it is spoken. "Calling him the Indian Killer doesn't make sense, does it?" she asks. "If it was an Indian doing the killing, then wouldn't he be called the Killer Indian?"

Walter and Alexie are friends and kindred spirits: they're both writers who veer between the realms of popular and literary fiction, both Spokane boys made good. Both take the stance of the outsider—because of being from Spokane, or because of starting as a genre writer, or because of growing up on a reservation, or because of being an Indian in the white literary world—which spurs them toward literary rebellion, writing books that are audacious, self-conscious, and messy. And the thriller is an inherently self-conscious form, whose formulas are so familiar that innovating on them is almost an imperative.

Like Alexie did in *Indian Killer*, with *Over Tumbled Graves*, Walter set out to challenge the thriller form, with his implied critique of familiar character types like the philosophical Dupree and the blowhard profilers. He is also denouncing the entire serial killer industry that the book could be a part of. In one scene, Caroline searches *serial killer* on the Internet and finds "eighty-six nonfiction books concerning serial killers currently in print," with titles advertising "'Amazing,' 'Evil' killers and 'Fantastic,' 'Bizarre' cases." She muses how a prostitute in Spokane "was worth a couple hundred bucks a day until her looks ran out or she died of AIDS or hepatitis or was shot by an angry john. But if this monster got hold of her, she could be a chapter in one of these books, perhaps even a composite character in the miniseries." *Over Tumbled Graves* hopes to be the serial killer book to end all serial killer books—literally.

As we hear more and more of the profilers' theories, it is striking how their process resembles that of fiction writers:

they probe intentions and motivations, building a character from the ground up. Only Caroline can see that they are not studying a person at all, but a superhuman character of their own creation, a dream nemesis who is inevitably a reflection of themselves. Late in the book, we learn that Blanton takes part in a practice that serial killers are famous for, keeping "trophies" from cases he worked on. It was "for research," he insists, that he took "some shell casings. Ransom notes. A pair of handcuffs . . . Some teeth." Caroline realizes the extent that the profilers have been profiling themselves, and the excitement and shame the killer's violence rouses in them. "She was alone in this, had always been alone," Caroline thinks with disgust. "Those men were investigating one crime and she was investigating another."

Like the dueling archetypes of Aristotle Little Hawk and the Indian Killer, both embodied in John Smith, these stories all reckon with the Janus nature of the cop and the bad guy. Randy Weaver and the FBI agents and U.S. marshals were eventually all Wild West outlaws. Serial killers and the investigators who look for them both exploit the bodies of vulnerable women. Blanton admits that he wants killers to be "evil" and "formidable," that they are "so much more interesting in the abstract than in reality." *Over Tumbled Graves* warns against magnifying killers' power in order to emphasize a duality between good and evil, to fabricate a worthy rival so one doesn't have to admit that one is encountering the worst of oneself. But it's an understandable temptation for investigators to view criminals as mythic opponents, to create a theory of violence that looks at the gun, not at where it's pointing. Because when you take away the monster, what are you left with?

The summer I turned thirteen, I read "The Trail to a Serial Killer" in *The Spokesman-Review* every day it came out, sitting at the psychedelic diner booth and looking out over our sloping yard at all of Moscow. Some details have clung to me, like the photograph of Melody Murfin's Mickey Mouse jacket, which Yates kept in his family's coat closet after he killed her. This was the first time I left the fairy tale of my childhood, or maybe the first time I understood it. That summer held for me both the full swell of puberty and my first depressive episode, when I stopped sleeping for a week and soothed my terror by watching infomercials all night. This was a rough initiation into womanhood, when I learned something fundamental about the place I was growing up in and its desperation and its remoteness. I learned that there were legions of hopeless women and they could be hurt and hidden so easily.

"The Trail to a Serial Killer" does good work to try to understand the stories of Yates's victims. They are all miserably similar: like that of Murfin, "a 43-year-old grandmother who first used drugs at 12, and couldn't give up the heroin she called her medicine. She bought it with the money she made selling sex." Or Michelyn Derning, "a former executive secretary who had moved to Spokane from Southern California a year earlier" and who also resorted to prostitution because of her drug addiction. Laurie Wason is described as "the devoted mother of a 12-year-old son until the summer before [she was killed], when she slid back into a heroin habit after six clean years." Almost as often as we hear about the victims' dire drug addictions, we hear about their children and grandchildren, the devoted mothers they strove to be in spite of their disease. Victim Shawn Johnson's mother is quoted as saying, "Both her boys just loved her more than anything."

Alongside these stories, it is even more galling just how many times authorities let Yates get away. He was stopped by police several times, once with a teenage prostitute in his car. During the investigation, Yates's teenage daughter came to the police department to report him for domestic violence. The police might have caught on sooner if they weren't so eager to avoid inconveniencing middle-aged, middle-class men—if, as police were subconsciously aligning themselves with him, Yates weren't also aligning himself with them.

At times during the investigation, police were convinced that one of their own was committing the murders, because of his practice of double tapping, or shooting victims twice, as police are trained to do. It turned out Yates was not a cop, but he had worked as a prison guard and was in the army for eighteen years. One volunteer in the investigation expressed disbelief that someone of Yates's long military experience could have committed these crimes. "It's hard to believe someone of that background, that rank, could be that sort of person," he said. But it was that kind of power and authority that Yates was drawn to: not something chaotic but something orderly. He wanted to control others and mete out punishment.

The end of "Trail to a Serial Killer" describes how Yates was not a problem prisoner. "He's a lot more deferential to authority, judges, than you might have from a twenty-year-old gangbanger who's trying to seize the high ground," the legal advisor to the Pierce County sheriff told the paper. But of course he identifies with authority figures—the out-of-control entitlement that leads one to commit such bold and depraved crimes would allow for nothing less. The real disease is that authorities prefer the banally evil Yates to the twenty-year-old gangbangers, the drug-addicted prostitutes. It's like we're back in an Old West settlement: with the prospectors, the robbers, the mountain men, the outlaws, the sheriff with his shiny badge, the judge far off in his courthouse. There are women at the brothel and the saloon, rumors of Indians hiding in the hills, but I'm not fooled. Even creekside with the earth folding itself into stark foothills, forest and mountain crags announcing the distance—even amid the anarchy, I know who's in charge.

The Husband Did It

It's always the husband. Just watch *Dateline*," Gillian Flynn writes in her novel *Gone Girl*, telling a public who gawked through the O. J. Simpson and Scott Peterson trials what they already know. Flynn's novel, along with David Fincher's 2014 movie adaptation, is the subversive American noir of the Court TV era. It features two remarkably odious narrators: Amy Dunne is cruel, self-important, and vindictive as she meticulously frames her husband for her own murder to punish him for cheating on her. Her husband, Nick Dunne, is self-pitying and self-deluded. Told by these two exaggerated voices, the story is a pulpy, shameless thriller, theatrical in every element, including its self-conscious interest in true crime television and the trope that spawned its premise: that a woman's husband is always the most logical suspect in her murder.

Amy watches shows about police procedure and reads true crime books to plan her stunt, luring Nick into doing classically suspicious things like taking out a life insurance policy on her. *Gone Girl* depicts the true crime obsession as a feedback loop—"Serial killers watch the same shows we do," one of the detectives says—and Amy sees in them a chance to transfigure herself. She becomes the author of her own narrative (literally, in the falsified diary that forms her early chapters of the novel), where she was "the hero, flawless and adored. Because everyone loves the Dead Girl."

What else could she gather from TV's proliferation of real life murder stories? Beginning with newsmagazine shows like *20/20* and *48 Hours*, with Court TV—originally a C-SPAN for salacious nineties court cases, which became popular during the trials of the Menendez brothers and O. J. Simpson—true crime TV is now reaching its gleeful, febrile, shameless apex. Reborn in 2008, the cable network Investigation Discovery is now all murder all the time. A sample of its programming: *Beauty Queen Murders*, *Catch My Killer*, *Deadly Devotion*, *Motives & Murders*, *Nightmare Next Door*, *Killer Clergy*, *Unusual Suspects*, and *Wives with Knives*.

If you watch enough hours of murder shows, you experience a peculiar sense of déjà vu: despite what would seem to be a wellspring of new cases, the same murders are recounted again and again across shows, migrating through Investigation Discovery programming blocks. The story of Florida airline gate agent Karen Pannell, who was murdered by her ex-boyfriend Timothy Permenter in 2003, has been on *Dateline*, *Forensic Files*, and the Investigation Discovery original program *Solved*. The most memorable fact of the case is that Permenter wrote *ROC*, the name of another of Pannell's exes, in her blood on the wall above her body, lamely attempting to forge a "dying declaration." This detail gives the story the feel of a whodunit. On *Dateline*, *Forensic Files*, and *Solved*, detectives emphasize the gruesome glamour of this clue, all saying in their interviews variations of "it's like something out of the movies."

It's a clue that announces itself, like the ones in Amy's sinister scavenger hunt in *Gone Girl* that lead Nick and the police to all the evidence she has planted. Amy orchestrates a truly grotesque melodrama, and still I find her more sympathetic than Nick, who is so convinced that he has tried, at every moment, to do the right thing. His father was an abusive misogynist, but Nick says, "I've tried all my life to be a decent guy, a man who loved and respected women, a man without hang-ups." When his issues with women do leak through, like when he becomes momentarily furious that a female detective is telling him what to do in his own home, he blames it on being raised by his father and thinks his self-awareness will absolve him. He is the classic male victim. Even his misogyny is something that was done to him.

This is why Nick's is the more damning characterization: because Amy bears no resemblance to any person who has ever walked the planet, but she bears a resemblance to women as conceived of in the nightmares of men like Nick, and there are many of those men walking the planet. For "decent" guys, comfortably vested with patriarchal authority, the nightmare is merely to be questioned, to no longer be the narrator of their own story. In *Gone Girl*, Flynn cracks open the American mainstream and lets Nick say one of our unsayable beliefs: that it is scarier for a man to be accused than to be killed.

The noir genre was born from the economic upheaval and disenfranchisement of Prohibition and the Great Depression, which relates closely to its function as, in the writer Sarah Nicole Prickett's words, "a grim and slippery indictment of American masculinity." When has the masculine fantasy (the American Dream?) been about anything other than control, about taking what's yours, in sex or in business? Prickett, in her brilliant *n+1* essay on the May 2014 massacre at UC Santa Barbara, "The Ultimate Humiliation," writes about the ways that violence against women is so often connected to men's professional and financial frustration. "It's hard not to think these killings might have been slowed, might even have been stopped," she writes of the Santa Barbara murders and others, "if more members of what is generously called 'the system' had the slightest acuity, maybe a little bit of feeling for a pattern, when it comes to fallen, immobilized men and their as-ever easiest targets."

In fact, identifying patterns is exactly what it takes to prevent domestic violence murders—and they can be prevented. The Amesbury, Massachusetts, Domestic Violence High Risk Team, founded in 2005, seeks specifically to prevent domestic violence homicide by coordinating the efforts of the various agencies that deal with aspects of domestic violence cases. A July 2013 *New Yorker* profile by Rachel Louise Snyder detailed their remarkable success in cutting the number of domestic violence homicides from one a year in Amesbury—a town of only 16,000 people—to zero. They have been so effective that the Obama administration studied them for its own initiative to reduce domestic violence. Team members try to disrupt the behavior of the abusers, rather than disrupting the lives of the victims by relocating them to shelters. They determine the risk that a domestic violence case will escalate to murder by looking for a number of red flags, including, tellingly, an abuser's chronic unemployment. Snyder describes how the risk of murder is closely correlated to moments of upheaval, "spiking when a victim attempted to leave an abuser, or when there was a change in the situation at home—a pregnancy, a new job." We hear in passing toward the end of the Karen Pannell episode of *Solved* that Timothy Permenter quit his job the day of her murder.

It is chilling how closely Pannell's murder mirrors the High Risk Team's warning signs for domestic homicide cases. She had broken up with Permenter a few weeks before; she told her family he had choked her and she was afraid of him; she called the police ten days before her murder because he was stalking her. (She also had a history of domestic violence with the boyfriend Permenter framed, though he assures the host of *Dateline*, "She gave as good as she got.") But on the murder shows, all these facts are elided or saved for the end of the episodes. At the beginning, it's all about the crime scene, the clues, and the giant letters written in Karen's blood on the wall. In fact, we hear the story of the murder as Permenter wanted it to be told.

On *Solved*, the detectives describe the change in Permenter after he realized he had not gotten away with Pannell's murder: "his demeanor . . . changed from this very cooperative, very talkative person to dark, quiet, angry person." Isn't that convenient? His demeanor reflects his depravity the moment they discover it. This kind of transformation must be a common sight for the legion of detectives and other authorities who still don't see the pattern. Snyder quotes from the coordinator of a group counseling organization for domestic abusers who emphasizes that abusers usually seem normal and even likable. Their partners become the focus for all their rage, so it rarely seeps into other areas of their lives. "I didn't hate and fear all women," Nick says defensively in *Gone Girl*. "I was a one-woman misogynist. If I despised only Amy, if I focused all my fury and rage and venom on the one woman who deserved it, that didn't make me my father." Aren't they all one-woman misogynists? When you consider that the Department of Justice claims that three women are killed by their partners every day, and according to the National Network to End Domestic Violence, domestic violence murders claimed 11,700 women between 2001 and 2012, it's no wonder that true crime fans roll their eyes at the predictability that the husband did it. Because it's not a mystery.

At the same time *Gone Girl* was blowing up in theaters, yet another cultural phenomenon was worrying over the received wisdom that the husband (or boyfriend) did it. On the flip side of *Gone Girl*'s sensational pulp was the meandering minutiae of the podcast *Serial*. In it, *This American Life* reporter Sarah Koenig delves with eccentric myopia into the details of a 1999 Baltimore murder case in which then eighteen-year-old Adnan Syed was convicted of killing his ex-girlfriend, Hae Min Lee. Koenig becomes particularly obsessed with the obvious inconsistencies in the story of the state's star witness, Adnan's friend

Jay, who claims he was enlisted by Adnan to help him bury the body. Koenig is disturbed by how much dishonesty and uncertainty the criminal justice system allows for before ceding reasonable doubt. She consults Jim Trainum, a former Washington, D.C., detective who now is an advocate for preventing false confessions. He acknowledges that while the inconsistencies in Jay's story are worrying, Koenig must also "look at the consistencies." In an interview with *The Intercept* after the podcast ended, the case's prosecutor, Kevin Urick, says essentially the same thing, insisting that witnesses rarely give a perfectly honest testimony, but that Jay's testimony on "material facts" was consistent and backed up by other evidence.

"The cops probably settled for what was good enough to be the truth," Trainum tells Koenig on *Serial*, and from Urick's statements, that is what happened, and it was probably what had to happen. Trainum's main warning to the police forces he trains is to watch out for verification bias—that is, looking only for evidence that fits their preconceived story of the crime. But that picking and choosing, the arranging of compelling details, is the very basis of our justice system: the case, which is not a compendium of all the evidence about an event, but a rhetorically convincing narrative of it. "Trials are won by attorneys whose stories fit," Janet Malcolm writes in *The Crime of Sheila McGough*, "and lost by those whose stories are like the shapeless housecoat that truth, in her disdain for appearances, has chosen as her uniform." Koenig recognized that the state's story of the crime was not the truth, but the shapeless, contradictory, and hopelessly incomplete truth she discovered did not satisfy her either.

It is easy to see why this tricky relationship to the truth is worrying: police and prosecutors' offices are powerful organizations that are heavily invested in maintaining an essentially unfair social order, and the presumption of innocence cannot be counted on to overcome juries' psychological biases. One of the more tone-deaf moments of Urick's *Intercept* interview is when he dismisses the notion that racism against people from the Middle East could have played a part in Adnan's conviction, saying, "This was well before September 11. Nobody had any misgivings about someone being Muslim back then." It is obvious that the prosecutors' story of the crime contained racist language and stereotypes. "He felt betrayed that his honor had been besmirched," Koenig quotes from Urick, as he sounds a racist dog whistle about the misogyny of Muslim culture. *Serial*'s crazy popularity may have had an implicit connection to the biggest news story of 2014, the wrongful lack of indictments in the cases of policemen who shot and killed unarmed black men, especially the murder of the St. Louis teenager Michael Brown, which sparked mass protests. Part of what was so baffling and depressing about those stories was the grand juries' refusal to even let the cases go to trial, as if it were important above all to preserve the image of who is a criminal and who is an authority. Clearly, there is damage done just by raising the question.

When a cop kills an unarmed man, it is because he senses his power being threatened by fear that he believes he should never have to feel. When a man kills his ex-girlfriend because she leaves him, he is saying the same thing: shame and sadness are feelings I should not have. Honor killings, as it turns out, are as American as apple pie. *Serial* is ultimately frustrating because it conflates a mistrust in unfair legal narratives with a mistrust in patterns that are all too real, namely "the most time-worn explanation for [a woman's] disappearance: the boyfriends, current and former." Skepticism about whether the husband did it shows a weird, classically American disdain for both authority and the powerless.

"Everyone loves the Dead Girl"—it's true. On *Dateline*, one of Karen Pannell's friends says that she was "pretty, smart, smiled all the time." At the end of the episode, the voice-over says that she "loved her friends, loved the beach, and died too young." On *Serial* we hear that Hae was athletic, outgoing, and funny, but after the second episode, where we hear excerpts from her diary, she disappears from her own story. From then on, it's all about Adnan and Jay, the evidence, the trial. But of course that's why we love her: because she's dead, and her death is the catalyst for the fun of sleuthing. It's why *Forensic Files* spends so much more time on debunking Permenter's obviously bogus clue, the message written in blood, than describing his history of abuse. I was more and more astonished reading the episode synopses from Netflix's *Forensic Files* collection: "When a woman's body is found in a burned-out house, microscopic clues on a piece of pipe help determine whether her death was an accident or murder." "When a woman is raped and murdered on the beach, investigators track down the killer through a pair of shoes left near the body." "At an apartment where a mother was stabbed to death, investigators find plenty of evidence but have no suspect to compare it against." It's clear we love the Dead Girl, enough to rehash and reproduce her story, to kill her again and again, but not enough to see a pattern. She is always singular, an anomaly, the juicy new mystery.

The Daughter as Detective

My parents met as library students at the University of Kentucky in 1979. From my intimate point of view, library school is a bit of an academic catchall, sometimes a plan B, appealing to weirdos of many backgrounds. People assume that librarians love books, but that isn't even it. University librarians like my parents love flying below the radar, omniscient about university curriculum but not bound by classroom teaching, grading, or even regular students. When she went to library school, my mom was a twenty-five-year-old polyglot, very pretty and shy, who until then had been taking graduate German courses and hanging around Lincoln, Nebraska, listening to the Who. My dad was thirty-two, starting a new career after years of working for the army as an Arabic translator. He is very loud and friendly, bubbly even. Contrary to the stereotype, he is a librarian who is constantly being shushed.

On their first date, he raced up the stairs to her apartment too enthusiastically and fell and broke his arm. He tried to deny that he had injured himself, and they went to a showing of *Casablanca*. He cradled his arm like a baby in the dark of the movie theater until the pain became too great, and my mom took him to the emergency room. The next day was Labor Day, and no pharmacies were open within walking distance of my dad's house. He didn't have a car, so he sheepishly called my mom to ask if she would drive him to get his prescription. She took him back to her house and made him grilled cheese and tomato soup.

The patently adorable and weird quality of their first date seems to have set the tone for their entire relationship. Early on, my dad gave my mom a copy of one of his favorite books: *Roseanna*, the first in a series of ten mystery novels by Swedish writers Maj Sjöwall and Per Wahlöö that follow the detective Martin Beck. "You'll find it ironic," he told her coyly, and she did: the title character, whose murdered corpse washes up on the shores of a Swedish lake, is a librarian in her twenties from Lincoln, Nebraska. My mom was not put off by the implications of this macabre coincidence, and she and my dad are still together now, many decades later. Improbably, my parents' marriage echoes the Dead Girl story, but with a happy ending.

Uncovering the origins of my dad's Martin Beck obsession has been more of a project than I first anticipated. When I asked how he discovered the books, he first told me that he read about them in a footnote in Robin Winks's 1969 essay collection *The Historian as Detective*, a study in the methods and pitfalls of the academic historian, imagining historians as sleuths solving thorny cases. Throughout the book, there are references to actual detective fiction, which my dad used as a syllabus. He talked to me at length about *The Historian as Detective*, but later was fuzzy on whether Winks had mentioned Sjöwall and Wahlöö at all. He was only certain that it was where he had heard about Robert Hans van Gulik's Judge Dee novels, historical mysteries about Tang Dynasty China. (The last Judge Dee mystery is called *Poets and Murder*, a possible alternative title for this book.)

When that lead dried up, he launched into a story from when he was in the army, working a desk job in Charlottesville, Virginia, and, as he told me, "having a lot of fun." Unexpectedly in 1973, he was called back from vacation and ordered to report to Fort Bragg. The Russians were in danger of joining the Arab-Israeli War, which might require reciprocal action from the United States. Nixon had put all of the 82nd Airborne, of which my dad was nominally a member, on alert. His superiors on the base refused to issue him a uniform because they didn't know how long he would be staying there. Instead of having him run in formation in street clothes, they sent him to the library and told him to read whatever he wanted. "I asked them whether they could teach me to jump out of an airplane if we had to go to the Middle East," he said of his time at Fort Bragg. "They told me, 'Eh, no problem.'" He read several of Sjöwall and Wahlöö's books there, but he was already very familiar with the series, so in the end they were not very important to that story.

A few days later, he called to tell me he actually first read the Martin Beck books when he was a student at the Defense Language Institute in Monterey, California. He had known he would be drafted and sent to Vietnam, so he joined the army and became an Arabic translator, an ironic way to avoid combat, considering our current geopolitical situation. In Monterey, he said, he had studied stupidly hard and had no fun, but he found a Martin Beck book on a rare trip into town. Later, he emailed me another confounding update: he visited a relative, a man named Jim who he claimed was his father's "cousin/nephew," the night Nixon had fired his attorney general. Jim had worked briefly in the Nixon White House, he told me. His stories unfold this way, full of the small, intriguing details that in a novel might work as foreshadowing. "I typically spent the first hour of the workday looking though *The Washington Post* to see what the latest Nixon news was," he went on to say before circling back. "I think I was at Jim's when I got a call instructing me to go to Fort Bragg."

I have found his stories often share an eccentric focus on what he was reading during his somewhat Forrest Gumpy journey through the twentieth century. Once he regaled me with memories of his time as a firefighter in Idaho in the late sixties, when he lived with an agriculture student who was later a prisoner in the Iran hostage crisis. (Rory Cochrane, the guy who played Lucas in *Empire Records,* portrayed Dad's roommate in the movie *Argo*.) Dad hitchhiked down to Jackson Hole during a day off and got *The Twenty-Seventh Wife,* Irving Wallace's biography of Ann Eliza Young, Brigham Young's wife, and Fawn Brodie's *No Man Knows My History: The Life of Joseph Smith the Mormon* from the library. He took issue with my saying in an early version of this essay that he checked out books about the Mormon Trail. "I was more interested in biography than the settler experience," he wrote me. "I have since read books like *Angle of Repose*, and taken an interest in TV shows like *Deadwood* and *Hell on Wheels*."

Maj Sjöwall and Per Wahlöö were a pair of Swedish journalists, a married couple who wrote the Martin Beck novels over long nights after their kids were asleep, working on alternate chapters. Their ten novels, released between 1965 and 1975, were an unexpected sensation, popular worldwide and the subjects of dozens of film and TV adaptations. The books are violent, sexually frank, and political, updating the hardboiled American noir for the liberal Scandinavian sixties. Nearly everyone acknowledges Sjöwall and Wahlöö as the origin point for Nordic noir, a regional genre that has produced international stars like Henning Mankell, Stieg Larsson, and Jo Nesbø. But Sjöwall and Wahlöö didn't just inspire other Scandinavian writers to embrace the murder mystery: they shaped the genre so completely that all of their descendants bear their eccentricities. The Martin Beck series is bizarre, a fitting starting point for what has become a multimilliondollar industry selling other bizarre, exasperating books.

The novels follow the melancholy detective Beck and his cohort in the Swedish National Police's Homicide Division as they solve cases including a serial sex murderer preying on children, a mass shooting on a bus, a "locked room" mystery involving a corpse decayed beyond recognition, and the assassination of the Swedish prime minister. Sjöwall and

Wahlöö's books hold very little allegiance to the typical noir that is sparsely written and pessimistic, showing one man against the world. Beck is the putative hero, but in practice the books are ensemble dramas, shading often into ensemble comedies. His colleagues are annoying misfits, described by their quirks, like the fastidious Fredrik Melander, who has a photographic memory, passionately loves his ugly wife, and spends too much time on the toilet. The series abounds with pairs of hapless bozos whose comedic value is underlined by their alliterative names. Bumbling beat cops named Kristiansson and Kvant wreak havoc at several crime scenes until Kristiansson is tragically killed. After that, Kvant gets a new partner named Kvastmo.

Sjöwall has said she and Wahlöö were influenced by "progressive" crime writers like Dashiell Hammett and Georges Simenon, but they took this progressive imperative rather further. Believing that "people read more mysteries than they do political pamphlets," they set out to write a Marxist indictment of the failures of the Swedish welfare state disguised as a series of mystery novels. They titled their series "The Story of a Crime"—that is, the crime of a cruel and unequal society. They described their political agenda as "the project," as if it were a covert mission of infiltration, when it could not have been more obvious. In book after book the authors include pages-long polemics about the nationalization of the police system, Stockholm's overdevelopment and the miseries of urban life, and the many demographics that had fallen through society's cracks. Their political tirades are written in a strident, journalistic tone, fissures where narrative conceit drops out completely. A visit to Beck's elderly mother becomes an occasion to bemoan (at length) the state of Swedish retirement homes:

> Nowadays they were called "pensioners' homes," or even "pensioners' hotels," to gloss over the fact that in practice most people weren't there voluntarily, but had quite simply been condemned to it by a so-called Welfare State that no longer wished to know about them. It was a cruel sentence, and the crime was being too old. As a worn-out cog in the social machine, one was dumped on the garbage heap.

My notes from the books are filled with comments like "So didactic" and, more to the point, "Why didn't somebody cut this?"

Critics revisiting Sjöwall and Wahlöö's books now are fawning, using that canonizing method of inverting their weaknesses instead of acknowledging them. A write-up in *The Wall Street Journal* from 2009 hilariously calls the Martin Beck books "anything but polemical." Louise France writes in *The Guardian* that while the action in the books is "often slow," they are addictive: "You want to block out a week of your life, lie to your boss, and stay in bed, gorging on one after another, as though eating packet upon packet of extra strong mints." I admit that I don't recognize the impulse to stay in bed for a week binging on mints, so maybe that's why I found the experience of reading these slow books a bit slower than France. The sometimes-tedious lack of action in the books is often pointed to as a strength. In his introduction to *Roseanna*, Henning Mankell writes that "it's probably one of the first crime novels in which time clearly plays a major role." Sjöwall echoed this idea recently, saying that "slowness, and the tension that waiting, distance, and irritating gaps in communication create, became an aspect of the books' realism." This argument smacks of imitative fallacy to me, but the wonky pacing of the series does point to its redeeming strength: the utter wonkiness and unconventionality of their entire approach.

Roseanna is more wrapped up in Dead Girl genre tropes than the rest of the books. At first the series seems less a treatise against corrosive changes in Swedish society than a darkly funny and melancholy meditation on the absurdity of Swedish bureaucracy. The novel opens by describing the administrative procedure for dredging the lake that eventually reveals Roseanna's body: it is unclear who can okay plans for dredging, and papers for it move among agencies, "passed from one perplexed civil servant to another," a process that takes months. This critique is more existential than political, a mirror for the frustration Martin Beck experiences in his marriage and his career. As a good Dead Girl should, Roseanna haunts and excites Beck, who for a time is unable to identify her. The case consumes him, so that "when he closed his eyes he saw her before him as she looked in the picture, naked and abandoned, with narrow shoulders and her dark hair in a coil across her throat." Once he identifies Roseanna, though, his image of her is inevitably complicated.

In conversations with her roommate and her boyfriend, back in Nebraska, Beck learns that she was promiscuous and odd, that she looked messy and slept with her friend's boyfriends. Where Beck thought he had found a Dead Girl, he had in fact found an ordinary dead woman.

Sjöwall and Wahlöö seem to take it upon themselves to demystify murder as much as possible, including clearing up the sanctifying haze that often obscures a victim. Some of the murderers in their books are so-called maniacs, but just as often seemingly maniacal crimes are only designed to look that way. The massacre on the city bus in *The Laughing Policeman* has the Swedish police looking at psychological profiles from American mass murderers. It turns out their villain is not like those madmen at all: he is a middle-class businessman who kills everyone on the bus to cover up his intended victim, a policeman who discovered another murder he committed years before. What Sjöwall and Wahlöö implicitly reveal is how much more disturbing this "logical" motive for the crime is than any insanity. The murderers in their books are desperate and disenfranchised people, bitter people seeking revenge, terrorists and organized criminals, all of whose motivations are understandable enough. It is refreshing how the authors of these mysteries do not seem to find crime very mysterious.

Sjöwall and Wahlöö's books at first seem to follow the Dead Girl genre's usual depiction of female sexuality as sinister and crazy. Women are constantly described as "nymphomaniacs," including Roseanna and other female victims, seemingly indicating that they have been punished for their insatiability. There are the requisite femmes fatales, many of whom make attempts to seduce Martin Beck, who distractedly rebuffs them—like many noir detectives, Beck is at first little more than a neutered intellect. But especially as the series wears on, we see that many of the regular characters have adventurous and unconventional sex lives, like Beck's detective friend who lives with his wife only on the weekends and has a girlfriend in Copenhagen. Beck releases himself from his unsatisfying marriage and finds new love with a magnetic and iconoclastic leftist. Unlike most detective series, which rely on the bleakness of their protagonists' lives, Sjöwall and Wahlöö allowed their detective a journey of enlightenment and redemptive love.

Sjöwall and Wahlöö did not have a conventional relationship either: Wahlöö was married when they met, and Sjöwall was twice divorced. They lived together for thirteen years but never legally married. Sjöwall has said that after Wahlöö died, shortly after the publication of the last Martin Beck novel, she was "kind of wild for a while. With guys, with pubs." She has had relationships since then but maintained her independence. "I know many guys," she said. "Some of them I have been together with for a while, some are just good friends. That is enough for me." Considering the authors' lifestyles, the books read as less judgmental of their promiscuous female characters. Despite my skepticism, I've come to believe Sjöwall and Wahlöö did what they set out to do: write a series of novels that are truly progressive, or, at least, that have fewer hang-ups.

My dad told me he had read the entire Martin Beck series "five or ten times." "Why?" I asked him. "Because I love them," he replied. I don't know why it's so frustrating that my dad refuses to say or even think about why he likes the things he does, when his preoccupations run so deep and are so consistent. When I ask him why he likes something, it's a perverse exercise less to gain new insight than to trick him into admitting to his personality. It's obvious to me why he likes the Martin Beck books. They are *exactly the kind of thing* he likes!

Although he has almost exclusively read mystery novels for my entire life, he has no taste for those with literary pretensions. He tells me he thinks he has read several Raymond Chandler novels, but they obviously did not make much of an impression. Stories about solitary, tortured heroes don't do it for him. He is into ad hoc teams like Sjöwall and Wahlöö's detectives, motley crews thrown together by circumstance and ennobled by their mission. Since he is a member of the first generation of modern nerds, it should be no surprise that he loves the valorous misfits that form the Rebellion in *Star Wars*. And in 1972, he turned down a fateful invitation to go to the rally where George Wallace was shot to stay home and watch Captain Kirk and his crew on *Star Trek*.

Before that, inevitably, there was *The Hobbit* and *The Lord of the Rings*, one of the enduring passions of his life. Because he is small and plucky, a lover of creature comforts but also an adventurer, my dad identifies with hobbits completely. When I was home to visit a few years ago, he knocked on my bedroom door to tell me he had chosen his "personal theme song": it was "Concerning Hobbits" from the *Lord of the Rings* soundtrack. "It makes my heart soar," he said. More intriguing is the typically opaque and bewildering story he told me once about how he and his friends would "run around in the woods with machetes" in order to "play hobbits." "How old were you?" I asked. "Oh, in college," he said. Learning about this proto-LARPing, I realized what a nerd pioneer he truly was.

The Martin Beck books also appeal to his enduring interest in bureaucracies and their dysfunctions. During his time working for the government, he was exposed to both secret missions and a lot of bullshit. Even today, if you ask him what he worked on there, he will cryptically tell you he was "assisting the defense attaché." In weaker moments he admits that he was helping translate intercepted Middle Eastern farming manuals to be sure they didn't contain Soviet propaganda. Later he got his master's in public administration, an experience that helped him realize he "didn't want to be a county supervisor" because his classes "made him want to die." As a child of a World War II veteran, he is particularly drawn to stories of antiauthoritarianism, of rebellious bureaucrats ignoring protocol to valiantly do the right thing. He frequently casts himself this way, bragging about arguing with a segregationist senator as a teenage student at Baylor or wearing a black armband to Nixon's second inauguration.

The last thing that all of his favorites have in common is more delicate to talk about, considering he is my father: his abiding love for any book, movie, or show with sexy parts. He has a truly childlike, if not innocent, avidity for graphic sex scenes and actresses' nipples. He, like Sjöwall and Wahlöö, is un-hung-up, an artifact of some sixties and seventies hippie campaign to cast sex as natural and healthy.

My mom brought this up when we were discussing his taste in movies. "'That has naked people in it,'" she said. "He says stuff like that all the time."

When I was a kid, the Martin Beck books were everywhere in my house, old duplicate copies my dad bought at garage sales and used-book stores, leering out at me with their incendiary titles: *Cop Killer. The Terrorists.* I had never read them until I began working on this book, when I read all of them over the course of several trying months, capping off that experience by reading another Swedish mystery series, the only one that has managed to supplant the Martin Beck books in my dad's heart: Stieg Larsson's *The Girl with the Dragon Tattoo* and its sequels, *The Girl Who Played with Fire* and *The Girl Who Kicked the Hornet's Nest,* collectively known as the Millennium series. I thought I was reading them in a quest to understand him better, but I'm not so sure that's true now. At worst, this essay seems like a Freudian patricidal project to ignore, then obsessively read, then talk shit in print about my dad's favorite books.

My dad's fixation on the Millennium series began so quickly and has held for so long it is stunning. He listened to the audiobooks on his iPod over and over again, until he reached the point where he would listen to their chapters on shuffle. I am admittedly inclined to be frustrated with Stieg Larsson's project, especially because after Larsson's idols Sjöwall and Wahlöö so cleverly subverted Dead Girl tropes, he embraced them. His books have the Dead Girl story's typical investigator with a good-guy complex, the crusading investi-

gative journalist Mikael Blomkvist, whose career is dedicated
to revealing fraud and corruption in the financial industry. In
the first book, he is drawn into solving the thirty-year-old disappearance of a wealthy industrialist's niece, Harriet Vanger.
The second and third have him trying to get to the bottom
of an ever deeper conspiracy that begins with the smuggling
of prostitutes from the Baltics and ends with a secret and all-
powerful cabal in Sweden's security police. Since Dead Girl
stories are so psychologically fraught, harried by every demon
Freud ever thought up, they often have the torturously complex plots of nightmares. The serial killer plot in the first book
particularly has that frenzied kitchen-sink feel: there is not one
but two killers, targeting scores of victims over many decades.
Some of the murders are humiliating and bizarre, inspired by
verses in Leviticus, and on top of this, the killers have ties to
nascent Swedish Nazi organizations.

The key element of any Dead Girl story is the investigator's haunted, semi-sexual obsession with the Dead Girl, or
rather, the absence that she has left. Larsson plays with this
overtly, as Blomkvist investigates Harriet Vanger's case and
he finds himself "hopelessly fascinated with the enigma of
the dead girl's disappearance." A police officer he talks to
also admits that he is still captivated by the Harriet Vanger
"puzzle." The implication of this choice of vocabulary, if I
am being uncharitable, could not be more clear: that women
are problems to be solved, and the problem of absence, a disappearance or a murder, is generally easier to deal with than
the problem of a woman's presence. True, Blomkvist (spoiler
alert) eventually finds Harriet alive and has an affair with

her, as he does with most of the women he comes into contact with in these novels, lending this Dead Girl story a stupefying and ambiguous denouement.

After Larsson's death, one of his hangers-on, the Swedish journalist Kurdo Baksi, wrote a strange hagiography of him for the *Daily Mail*, in which he discusses Larsson's passionate opposition to violence against women. When they discussed this violence, Baksi writes, "Stieg's eyes would fill with tears. He could not accept someone could be denied their freedom simply because of their gender." Larsson's disgust at what he saw as a ubiquitous misogyny was supposedly the impetus for the Millennium series, with the original Swedish version of the first novel being titled *Men Who Hate Women*. But forgive me if I find the books to be something less than the feminist treatises they claim to be. As Christopher Hitchens wrote in his characteristically rude piece on Larsson, their "moral righteousness comes in very useful for the action of the novels, because it allows the depiction of a great deal of cruelty to women, smuggled through customs under the disguise of a strong disapproval."

More troubling to me than the books' violence is a flaw at the core of Larsson's anti-misogynist mission. Throughout the novels, characters insist that "men who hate women" are not monsters: they are everyday people. Blomkvist's fellow investigator, Lisbeth Salander, says in the first book that their villain is "not some insane serial killer . . . he's just a garden variety bastard who hates women." But Larsson's villains are as monstrous as he can make them, even though they may hide in plain sight. They are cruel, insatiable, and meticulous, with strange and deviant sexual appetites. The first book is obsessed with sexual sadism, ending with a flourish in a serial killer's tricked-out torture chamber. This depiction sidesteps the complicated truth of sexual desire and fantasy, which is that in certain circumstances, a person can be turned on by the idea of violence that they would never commit or condone. In the same way, the books sidestep the true face of misogyny: if men who hate women are normal and common, then misogynist violence does not have to be so diabolical. Larsson's partner, Eva Gabrielsson, has said that Larsson was inspired by comic books, and he obviously could not resist the temptation of the archvillain, a worthy foe for his hero. Where Sjöwall and Wahlöö succeeded in deromanticizing crime and criminals, in his mission to condemn violence against women, Larsson has ended up lionizing its perpetrators by exaggerating the same old prudish tropes.

The first Millennium series novel features what is in my eyes a maddeningly long final act, where Blomkvist, having solved the mystery of Harriet Vanger's disappearance, seeks revenge on a corrupt Swedish billionaire who has sidelined his career. Later I came to see that this fight against corruption was exactly the point of Larsson's books, with misogyny functioning more as an occasional thematic hobbyhorse. Larsson was a lauded investigative journalist, having founded the anti-fascist *Expo* magazine, and his plots about corruption among CEOs and government agents gave him the opportunity to write random op-eds a la Sjöwall and Wahlöö on subjects including the injustice of the stock exchange, the

Swedish police force's use of hollow-point bullets, and incon-sistencies in enforcing prostitution laws.

In fact, twisted misogyny often acts as a metaphor for other kinds of personal corruption, with fascism, authoritarian overreach, and greed manifesting as sexual malignancy. The political intrigue Blomkvist is investigating in the second and third books turns out to be a conspiracy of perverts, as a sadistic rapist lawyer, a security agent who consorts with pros-titutes, and a pedophile psychiatrist conspire to get Salander institutionalized. Blomkvist and Salander hack the hard drive of the psychiatrist, Peter Teleborian, and discover masses of child pornography. This evidence is sprung upon him during his testimony against Salander in the third book, and he is led in handcuffs from the courtroom. After that, as if caught off guard by the implausibility of the book he has found himself in, the judge remarks, "I have never even heard of a case in which the prosecutor's chief witness is arrested during a court in session." My dad told me that the downfall of Peter Tele-borian is "one of the great moments in literature."

If I sound completely fed up with Larsson's books, it's be-cause I have barely talked about Salander, the girl of the books' titles, who is undeniably their soul and their selling point. When Blomkvist first meets her, she is working as a private investigator at a firm called Milton Security, a role she dispatches so brilliantly, we later learn, because she is one of the most skilled hackers in Sweden, as well as a polymath with a photographic memory. The books are as preoccupied with her unusual appearance as with her unusual talents: she is very small and looks very young, with tattoos, piercings, and a personal style that could be approximated as motorcycle Goth.

Larsson is seemingly in love with the trick of having his heroine judged as a child, a criminal, a deviant, only to have her prove everyone wrong with her unbelievable intellect. The longest arc of the novels is correcting the injustice she suffered from Sweden's guardianship system. She was put in a mental hospital as a child, and when she was released was assigned a guardian within the government who had control of her legally and financially. An incorrect psychological assessment from when she was a teenager had the government believing she was mentally ill, with criminal tendencies and very low intelligence. Her edgy appearance did nothing to persuade the guardianship agency of her competency.

But despite the Millennium series' focus on Salander's journey to seize self-determination, she is often constrained by the narrative's own gaze, even when it is mediated through characters who will end up in the wrong. Descriptions of her are icky either in their prurience or disgust, with a creepy focus on her body. In the first book, I count six times where she is described as looking anorexic (she is not anorexic). Before we have gotten to know her at all, several pages are devoted to her boss's coming to terms with his sexual attraction to her, a plot element that goes exactly nowhere. She later jumps into bed with Blomkvist, as she is (conveniently) into older men. Salander is, in many ways, a male fantasy of a rebel girl: she is bisexual, rides a motorcycle, works out at a boxing gym, and eats only junk food. Considering that she is only one of Blomkvist's many paramours, her characterization works especially to distinguish her from his other girlfriends. As with so many detective series, the Millennium series seems to be a study in every kind of woman the detective, as proxy for the writer, could possibly be attracted to.

Luckily, Salander is a more compelling, surprising, and complex character than Blomkvist, in his possessive and protective desire, can see. Salander, a classic avenging angel, has her own notion of justice, but it is hard to rationalize her actions, as Blomkvist repeatedly does, as stemming from some deep morality. She uses her computer skills to steal millions from the corrupt industrialist at the end of the first book because he is a bad guy, but also because the opportunity presents itself. When she was twelve years old, she attempted to kill her abusive deadbeat father by throwing a burning bottle of gasoline into his car. This violence is constantly justified by Blomkvist and others, who say that she was only trying to protect her mother, but I do wonder if she could have protected her in a way that did not involve a firebomb.

Larsson created a character so interesting that she wriggled from the grasp of his narrative, letting ambiguity and chaos into a world he set up as black-and-white, good guys versus bad. Eva Gabrielsson often speaks about the books like sacred tracts, seeing them as being didactic first, entertaining second. I would tend to agree. But with Salander, who is impulsive, intransigent, and sad, very often unable to be there for the people she cares about most, it is difficult to say what lesson is to be learned—fortunately for the reader.

Without her, we would have only Blomkvist, a character as intolerably, triumphantly decent as Perry Mason. (Mason, the hero of Erle Stanley Gardner's legendary detective series, is the smuggest, most well-adjusted milquetoast in the history of mysteries. In the early nineties, my dad recorded every episode of the *Perry Mason* TV series onto VHS tapes and cataloged them on our old DOS-prompt computer.)

Salander injects into Larsson's matrix of morals some of the anarchy of children's literature, and that was by design. Gabrielsson explains how Salander was inspired by Pippi Longstocking:

> This delightful and formidable little girl has been a champion of equality between the sexes: she doesn't depend on anyone, can use a revolver, has sailed the seven seas. . . . But the main thing about Pippi is that she has her own ideas about right and wrong—and she lives by them, no matter what the law or adults say.

But Salander lends some of the melancholy of children's literature, too. Pippi's story, after all, is not only about how she brings excitement to a staid Swedish village, but the problem of her loneliness, as she seeks friendship and understanding in a world that wasn't made for her.

I am charmed by Gabrielsson's description of Pippi Longstocking, not only because it describes the near-superhero Salander so well, but because in spirit (though in not many practical details), it describes my dad, too. I always think of him as an impish mischief-maker, something of a manic pixie dream dad, whistling in public, sobbing at stories on NPR, flirting with babies, buying candy and stuffed animals, and generally pissing off uptight assholes. Once when he was walking with my brother, they saw a car with a "Who is John Galt?" bumper sticker, a reference to Ayn Rand's *Atlas Shrugged*. He stuck a notecard on the windshield that said YOU ARE AN IDIOT.

As I think about my dad and Pippi, it illuminates another common feature of the films, books, and TV that he likes: girls who kick butt. He was an early fan of *Buffy the Vampire Slayer* (though he believes it took a downturn after she graduated from high school) and is even more ardently committed to the cult teen detective show *Veronica Mars*, whose plucky heroine wields a Taser almost as well as Salander does. I first told him to watch *Veronica Mars*, and later, after he had breathlessly emailed me about Veronica and Logan and Dick Casablancas enough times, I regretted ever watching it. I used to think that he only had some embarrassing pervy attraction to girls who kick butt, and, I mean, he definitely does. But after he told me through tears that he "only wants Veronica to be happy," I should have gotten the picture that he sees himself in them, too. I guess it is no surprise that he identifies with teenage girls, when there is an illustrious tradition of grown men expertly crafting young women's entertainment, from boy bands of all eras to *Sixteen Candles* and *Pretty in Pink* to, indeed, *Buffy* and *Veronica Mars*.

"I definitely think he relates to those girls," my mom told

me. She reminded me of a scene at the end of the first Millennium series book, when Salander realizes she has fallen in love with Blomkvist and resolves to confess her feelings to him. When she finds him, he is on a date with another woman, and Salander is crushed. This is the most affecting part of the books for my dad, my mom told me. "He'll just cry and cry about that part," she said. All along I thought he saw himself as the valiant everyman Blomkvist, who comes to the aid of the sexy girl who kicks butt. I was wrong about that, and I shouldn't make the mistake of thinking I have figured him out again. I told him that I thought he identified more with Blomkvist, but then it occurred to me that he maybe identified with Salander. "I don't think I'm like any of them," he told me stubbornly. "I just think the books have the ring of realism," a description that in my opinion could not be more incorrect.

When I complained to my mom about my dad describing books that strain plausibility in every way as having "the ring of realism," she explained to me how this is one of the phrases he uses indiscriminately to describe works that grab his imagination (the other is "the spark of greatness") in the manner of, for instance, the cop show *Hill Street Blues*. This shorthand praise is another way for him to avoid analyzing his own whims. It's also, maybe, a defensive posture to keep us from analyzing him.

This could be why I have delayed addressing what was supposed to be one of the points of this essay: whether my dad has autism and if it matters. The therapist he works with has suggested that he has Asperger's syndrome, based on his difficulty reading conversational cues and other people's moods; his short temper; his many intense enthusiasms; and his almost complete lack of social inhibition, which often leads to totally inappropriate behavior. When I asked him about it for this essay, it was the first time we had ever spoken about it. "Why are you asking me about *that*?" he said incredulously, and I explained that it made me think of him when Blomkvist privately guesses that Salander has Asperger's because of her savant-like skills and social awkwardness. "Yes, that is one possible diagnosis," he said about Salander. Of his own diagnosis, he would only say, oddly, that he didn't remember it, comparing it to the apparent amnesia he developed in the 1990s when he had bursitis of the elbow. I pressed him, but he stood by his "no comment." "I have zero memory of anyone ever saying I have Asperger's," he said. "I'd completely forgotten that and I hadn't thought about it. I don't have any thoughts or any opinions."

I really don't blame him for having no thoughts or opinions. No one even raised the possibility that he was on the autism spectrum until he was sixty-eight, and charging someone that age with a condition we often associate with childhood is complicated by a lifetime of ambiguities and examples to the contrary. As he approached his eighth decade, the methods he had learned to navigate the world were just his personality, as they are, I assume, for everyone. He was also unwittingly encountering a fateful tendency in my family to monumentalize the eccentricities of its members, to talk and laugh about them among ourselves and with strangers—write about them, even—until the picture shifts into focus, and those eccentricities reveal themselves as dysfunction.

And no matter his age, I've come to see autism spectrum diagnosis as an alienating thicket, where there is no textbook case. At his therapist's suggestion, he read David Finch's memoir *The Journal of Best Practices*, the story of Finch being diagnosed with Asperger's as an adult and using this new self-knowledge to become a better husband. Despite what would seem to be obvious commonalities between Finch and my dad, he found no applicable lessons in his story, and he thought the book made Finch look, frankly, like a jerk. Finch and his wife, Kristen, were on an episode of *This American Life* in 2012, where Kristen, a speech therapist who worked with disabled kids, says that she and her coworkers would always joke that their husbands were autistic. The stereotypes in that joke are uncomfortable for me in both directions. Joking about men's emotional stuntedness seems at best inaccurate, at worst self-reinforcing, and joking about autistic people as socially retarded and robotic almost certainly increases their ostracization. But it also collapses the almost endless variation among people with autism spectrum disorders: my dad didn't recognize Finch's compulsions, which isn't to say he has none of his own.

I found myself combing through websites about the autism spectrum, many of which are compiled by civilians who have the disorder themselves, who I think are also trying to come to terms with the many ways one can have autism. One particular website called Inside Perspectives of Asperger Syndrome and the Neurodiversity Spectrum describes possible autism spectrum symptoms across an exhaustive list of categories, including work, sex, eating, sleep, phone problems, "spacing out," and even allergies and drug sensitivities. The primary sources on every page are testimonials from web users who identify as having autism and related conditions, like Asperger's and ADHD, describing their own experiences. Many of these don't describe my dad at all, while others do with eerie accuracy. During the conversation we had about his possibly being autistic, this description was dinging in my head: "Some have problems with reciprocity & timing and either talk on and on without letting anyone else get a word in edgewise, constantly interrupt others without realising that it's disrespectful to do so, or say nothing at all unless asked a direct question." There is of course also the claim that many with autism "are able to hyper-focus intently on the same thing for hours, days, sometimes weeks on end, and keep up a special interest for years"—see Sjöwall, Wahlöö, Larsson, et al.

One of the most helpful things I read on Inside Perspectives is this eloquent description from one of the site's users of the problem with seeing autism as a disorder:

> If you have one neurodiverse trait you are more likely to have additional neurodiverse traits. I am not sure why this is. The more of these traits you have, the more difficult it is to function . . . If you can't function in society because you have too many of these traits and/or they are too intense then it becomes a disability. And when it becomes

a disability then they have to put a label on it. . . .
The 'clump traits together and give them a name'
strategy is fundamentally [*sic*] flawed . . . Labeling
falsely claims you have one thing, not a group of
things which may be better treated individually.

But viewing the autism spectrum as a matrix of possible
traits evokes all the problems of mental health diagnosis,
because, to put it simply, everyone has traits. The American
Psychiatric Association's *Diagnostic and Statistical Manual
of Mental Disorders* (*DSM*) does not seek to describe what a
healthy person looks like: psychological "normalcy" is judged
only by an absence of any of the dysfunctions it addresses.
Considering the gargantuan length of the *DSM*, there are
nearly as many ways to be crazy as there are to be alive. But
despite the *DSM*'s attempt at exhaustiveness, it remains very
difficult to wrangle a human being's habits, thoughts, desires,
quirks, and pain under the heading of a single diagnosis of
mental illness. This is underlined by the manual's primary use,
which is not therapeutic, but clerical: a diagnosis of a disorder
with a *DSM* classification is often the requirement for an insurance company to authorize treatment.

I gained the most insight from the wonderful autistic
writer and rhetorician Melanie Yergeau, who discusses the
problem of diagnosis on her blog autistext.com. As she
writes, "For many, diagnosis is validating and/or leads to
self-understanding. Diagnosis can explain a lot." But a disease model of autism, where there are degrees of severity and
some have it "worse" than others, effaces the individual value

of autistic people. Yergeau writes powerfully for the model of disability that relies on disabled people's rights to advocate for their own needs:

> Whether your disabled child screams in the grocery checkout line or testifies in front of Congress, he is self-advocating. Whether your disabled child throws peas in your face or writes a snarky blog post or falls asleep during board game nights or says NO in all capital letters, she's self-advocating. And none of these things is less noble or gutsy than the other.

All people have needs that flow from their humanity, not from a predetermined list of problems that we call disability. Diagnosis and the vocabulary that it trades in should be tools to help people understand themselves and ask for what they need. It follows, then, that if the language of disability doesn't help someone advocate for himself or herself, he or she should be free to reject it.

For my dad, navigating the "neurodiverse traits" that make functioning more difficult individually—like helping him to remember not to make too much noise around the house, to reflect more on his emotions, not to give in so quickly to frustration—is most helpful, and it doesn't require him to align all the vagaries of his personality with a diagnostic label. The autism designation isn't helpful for him. The autism spectrum is one more place I've looked for my dad, with only partial success. My mom told me that, library cataloger that she is, one of her greatest interests is in creating typologies, finding categories and seeing where things fit. But she has never been that good at categorizing the people close to her, not suspecting that there was anything in my dad's weirdness that might be explained by someone else's weirdness. "I tend to be accepting of the way that people are," she told me helplessly, which might be another way of saying that love is blind.

Larsson died of a heart attack shortly after delivering the manuscript for *The Girl Who Kicked the Hornet's Nest*, never living to see his novels published, much less the worldwide sensation they would become. Per Wahlöö died after he and Sjöwall finished the tenth Martin Beck novel, blessedly missing most of the social degradation he had warned against. These deaths are both eerie in the same way: socially conscious writers not living to know how right they were. Sjöwall cheerily admits now that "the project" was a failure. "Everything we feared happened, faster," she told *The Guardian* in 2009. "People think of themselves not as human beings but consumers. The market rules, and it was not that obvious in the 1960s, but you could see it coming." What would have been harder for them to see coming was the murder of the Swedish prime minister Olof Palme in 1986, eleven years after they wrote about a fictional Swedish prime minister being assassinated in *The Terrorists*.

The most remarkable thing about reading the Millennium series now, in the spring of 2017, is their overwhelming, prophetic resonance with the scandals of the 2016 election and the Trump administration, as they involve neofascists, computer hackers, sexual misconduct scandals, Russian spies, government corruption, evil billionaires, and journalistic integrity. It makes me wish Larsson had lived to comment on it, although I assume the current era would immediately make him wish he were dead.

Many people have noted the marketing brilliance of changing the title of Larsson's *Men Who Hate Women* for the English translation, shifting the focus from creepy men to always more salable "girls." *Men Who Hate Women* could be another alternate title for my book, and I have chosen, maybe hypocritically, to sell it on girls instead. In the end, the careers of Larsson and Sjöwall and Wahlöö turn out to be Dead Man stories, where men leave their wives and collaborators to deal with their absence for decades. This female survival is probably the truer story and, I think Larsson, Sjöwall, and Wahlöö would agree, a better one, but it doesn't have the same addictive glamour that comes with a Dead Girl. In *Roseanna*, one of Beck's colleagues mentions a movie that the suspect they're trailing goes to see. "It has a wonderful ending," he says. "Everyone dies except the girl."

Larsson died at fifty, after years of working too much, eating too much junk food, drinking too much coffee, and smoking too many cigarettes. There has been extended drama involving his partner of thirty years, Gabrielsson, who, since they never legally married and Larsson left no will, is not entitled to any of his posthumous millions. His death was ironic and unjust, having happened at altogether the wrong time. I can't help but think about my dad when I read about Larsson's heart attack: how Larsson's colleagues found him in a chair, breathing heavily and in a cold sweat, and even then he did not want to admit he was sick. My dad was probably in congestive heart failure for weeks before my brother and his boyfriend found him hunched over in a parking lot, gasping for air. I burst into terrified tears when I saw him on a gurney in the emergency room, looking so gray and puny. "It makes me cry, too," he said and sobbed.

Insofar as this is a Dead Girl story with a happy ending, you know that my dad got better. His cardiac emergency became another episode in his life, another story underscored, appropriately, by reading. In the hospital after his angioplasty, he had a paradoxical reaction to a sedative that launched him into an hour-long panic attack. Every sixty seconds, he would jump out of bed and run around his hospital room, endangering his fresh stitches. At one point my mom, her nerves completely shot, picked up *The Girl Who Kicked the Hornet's Nest* and began to read from Salander's trial. This was the only thing that soothed my dad, and she read to him until he fell asleep.

Part 2

Lost in Los Angeles

There There

When I turned twenty-five, I lived in Los Angeles. That is, I was in Los Angeles, and I was, ostensibly, alive.

I don't know what else you call it when you come to Los Angeles but then your job prospects fall through and you have to survive on your wits and your friends' couches and your birthday money.

I had never even been to California before I decided to move there. As I drove down from the Sierra Nevada foothills on Highway 20 ("The 20"?) toward my aunt and uncle's house in the northern Sacramento Valley, I found myself exclaiming out loud to no one, "Look, a palm tree!" Because I grew up in Idaho, my entire frame of reference for California was as a place people left to retire in the Northwest, and as vaguely fancy. I still have difficulty shaking that last idea. When I discovered I didn't get cell phone service in my aunt and uncle's house, I could only think, outraged, "In *California*?"

My more recent frame of reference for California comes from books, which tend to paint it as a sun-drenched and contradictory collection of tropes revolving clumsily around a nonexistent center. Joan Didion has devoted at least a portion of each of her four essay collections to trying to understand California, and she spends all of her 2004 book *Where I Was From* parsing the state's contradictions. "This book represents an exploration into my own confusions about the place . . ." she writes early in *Where I Was From,* "misapprehensions and misunderstandings so much a part of who I became that I can still to this day confront them only obliquely." These misunderstandings are mostly related to the way that California's imagination of itself—as native, independent, and wild—is at odds with what has from the beginning been its essential character: it is immigrant, corporate, and overdeveloped. As Didion writes, "A good deal about California does not, on its own preferred terms, add up," or, as she quotes from W. B. Yeats in the epigraph to her first essay collection, *Slouching Towards Bethlehem,* "The center cannot hold."

Or as my cousin Tony told me in a dark comedy club in Santa Monica, "There is no there there." This might be Gertrude Stein's most Gertrude Steiny quote, but it is not that sphinxlike when taken in context. She was describing how she felt when revisiting her childhood home in Oakland: the loss one can feel for a place when its fundamental character has been so changed that, while it isn't gone, it is not exactly *there* either.

But Stein's koan works just as well when describing the literal and existential decentralization one experiences in Los Angeles. I missed three-quarters of the show that night, including Tony's set, because I couldn't find the club. I wandered dumbfounded around Santa Monica's prefab "promenade," two sterile streets of luxury storefronts and chain restaurants, passing the same stores again and again, until I realized that I had actually been circling around the club—it was tucked in an alley, the entrance to which could be found, I was told later, because it is "near the Hooters."

I was in a poisonous mood when I drove to West Hollywood, bought Raymond Chandler's 1949 novel *The Little Sister* at Book Soup, and went to a Thai restaurant across Sunset to sullenly stare at its cover and eat noodles. In it I found private detective Philip Marlowe at his most bitchy and pessimistic. "I'm just sitting here because I have no place to go," he tells a client. "I don't want to work. I don't want anything."

Probably a majority of the appeal of Chandler's novels revolves around Marlowe, a jaded and impossibly savvy outsider whose general disdain for women makes him irresistible to them. "What a way you have with the girls," the beautiful movie star Marlowe is working for in *The Little Sister* says to him. "How the hell do you do it, wonderful? With doped cigarettes? It can't be your clothes or your money or your personality." How Marlowe does it is certainly a valid question. In the world of Chandler's fiction, the answer mostly lies not with him but with the women: they are craven, sex-obsessed, and ambitious, qualities Marlowe has learned to expect and play to. I find this pattern fascinating: Chandler's novels are so misogynistic that the resentments they betray veer back in on themselves, pointing toward a complex in Marlowe.

Marlowe's ambivalent sexuality always becomes a mechanism of the novels' plots: if he is attracted to a woman—whether she is beautiful or plain, seemingly worldly or innocent—it means she is troubled, hiding dark secrets, and quite probably amoral and dangerous. In *The Little Sister*, he is enlisted by a nerdy and prudish teenager from Manhattan, Kansas, named Orfamay Quest to track down her older brother. Marlowe finds her corny and uptight, and she can offer him only twenty dollars for his services, but he still takes the case. "I was just plain bored with doing nothing," Marlowe says to explain why he agreed to work for her, but then he adds, "Perhaps it *was* the spring too. And something in her eyes that was much older than Manhattan, Kansas."

Marlowe chases this glimmer of sex in Orfamay's eyes, stealing a kiss from her along the way to discovering that she is involved with blackmailing her sister and murdering her brother. Heterosexual relationships are dangerous: one must balance the necessity of sex with the impossibility of trust. In fact, one of Marlowe's only positive relationships in all of Chandler's fiction is with a man, Terry Lennox, in *The Long Goodbye*. Like with his female paramours, Marlowe finds himself strangely drawn to Lennox, a war hero and alcoholic who has been accused of murdering his wife. Marlowe helps Lennox flee to Mexico and ends up going to jail for him. Although Marlowe has mixed feelings about the lengths he goes to protect Lennox, he is more purely devoted to him than to any of the women he is sexually involved with. At times Marlowe makes me think of Patricia Highsmith's great sociopathic hero, Tom Ripley. But the connection between Ripley's emotional problems and the horrors he is driven to commit is spelled out more plainly: it is closeted homosexuality pushed to pathology.

Of course, Chandler is also just participating in the noir genre's greatest trope: the femme fatale. In detective stories, the femme fatale appears as seductive and seemingly helpless, when she is in fact self-serving, traitorous, and possibly bloodthirsty. It is a trope that reveals a deep fear of women and sex. There is the fact that many of these women are described as nymphomaniacs: for instance, the sex-crazed and deranged younger Sternwood daughter in *The Big Sleep*, and, in *The Little Sister*, the sultry, sinister film star Dolores Gonzales. "You always wear black?" Marlowe asks Gonzales. "But yes. It is more exciting when I take my clothes off," she replies. "Do you have to talk like a whore?" he says. "I wear black because I am beautiful and wicked—and lost," Gonzales eventually explains, in one of the more breathtakingly obvious descriptions of a femme fatale in all of literature.

Some femme fatales knowingly use their sexuality to get ahead. "I do not draw a very sharp line between business and sex," Gonzales says in *The Little Sister*. "Sex is a net with which I catch fools." But others are unconsciously, mysteriously driven to ruin and manipulate men, modern sirens enticing them to rocky shores. This is the case with Faye Greener in Nathanael West's great Los Angeles novel *The Day of the Locust*. She is a shallow and amoral teenage actress who inspires every male character in the novel with a crazy, infuriating desire. "She lay stretched out on the divan with her arms and legs spread, as though welcoming a lover, and her lips were parted in a heavy, sullen smile," West writes, describing a photograph Faye has given the book's protagonist, Tod Hackett. "She was supposed to look inviting, but the invitation wasn't to pleasure."

The Day of the Locust is a deeply, almost hysterically misogynistic book. The men in it are desperate to physically control and punish Faye, purely because of the desire she elicits in them. This male paranoia in West's and Chandler's work does seem related to their vision of Los Angeles as alien territory ruled by no knowable order. The fact that women in Los Angeles could be deceitful, ambitious, and in control confirmed it as a kind of bizarro-world—and confirmed that any hero who braved its borders, no matter how many Los Angeles eccentrics surrounded him, was truly alone.

I was staying in Long Beach with my friend James and his brother, John, in their bachelor pad furnished only with two deck chairs, two air mattresses, a forty-two-inch flat-screen television, and an inflatable raft for a sofa. James and John were both railroad conductors, and they worked insane hours: they got called in to work in the middle of the night, and every trip, they would be gone for days at a time. I was sitting around their apartment alone one night when I came across *The Big Lebowski* in a pile of DVDs. I had somehow never seen it, so I put it on the big screen and settled in on the raft.

The movie's slacker hero, the Dude, is drawn into a kidnapping case in which a millionaire with the Dude's same name, Jeff Lebowski, asks him to track down his nymphomaniac (!) wife. As he unravels the mystery, he has encounters with various Hollywood weirdos. The Dude is a league bowler, unemployed, and terminally laid back, but just like Philip Marlowe, trouble finds him. In fact, I was struck by how much of *The Big Lebowski* was reminiscent of Chandler, an insight that, it turns out, is either pretty perceptive or totally obvious. In the second paragraph of the movie's Wikipedia article, I learned that the Coen brothers had "wanted to do a Chandler kind of story—how it moves episodically, and deals with the characters trying to unravel a mystery, as well as having a hopelessly complex plot that's ultimately unimportant."

The Big Lebowski is infused with Western genre elements, like its mysterious cowboy narrator who waxes folksy at the beginning and end of the film and shows up twice at the bowling alley bar to order a sarsaparilla. The Dude's nickname brilliantly recalls both the cowboys of the Old West and the stoners of the New West. Los Angeles has a strange dual relationship to the cowboy, given that cowboys were a real part of the history of Southern California and California is still an agricultural state, but Hollywood also created and propagated the John Wayne/Lone Ranger archetype. It's the mess of reality and fantasy embodied by the buckaroos in *The Day of the Locust*, who live in real cowboy camps in the canyons surrounding L.A. but make a living by playing extras in Westerns.

It seems the Los Angeles of Chandler, West, and the Coen brothers still retains something of the frontier feeling that has defined the myth of the American West. It is dominated by settlers and transplants, prospectors trying to strike it rich, and the rules can always be rewritten. This is why the hero always finds himself interloping on ever-stranger pockets of the Los Angeles population: in Chandler, it's movie stars, drug dealers, and gangsters. In *The Day of the Locust*, it's cowboys, cockfighting midgets, old vaudeville clowns, and Hollywood madams. In *The Big Lebowski*, it's millionaires, conceptual artists, German nihilists, and pornographers. These stories riff on what has always been sold as the American frontier's most attractive and most terrifying quality: anything can happen.

West understood this mandate for reinvention when he said with tongue in cheek that he changed his name from Nathan von Wallenstein Weinstein following Horace Greeley's famous enjoinder, "Go West, young man." But this potentiality also knocks our Los Angeles heroes perpetually off-balance, keening in astonishment and disgust at what God hath wrought. West describes Los Angeles's manic architectural sensibilities in *The Day of the Locust*: "Only dynamite would be of any use against the Mexican ranch houses, Samoan huts, Mediterranean villas, Egyptian and Japanese temples, Swiss chalets, Tudor cottages, and every possible combination of these styles that lined the slopes of the canyon." Chandler, in his descriptions, moves beyond West's exhaustion to disdain when he talks about "the luxury trades, the pansy decorators, the Lesbian dress designers, the riffraff of a big hard-boiled city with no more personality than a paper cup."

As I took the 405 from Long Beach to Carson to Hawthorne to Inglewood to Mar Vista to Culver City, then east on the 10 to Mid-City and downtown, doubling back on the 101 through Chinatown to Echo Park to Silver Lake to Koreatown to Hollywood to West Hollywood to Beverly Hills, I was impressed by the unnerving sense of a city that sprang up overnight and sprawled like an invasive species over the landscape. "There ought to be a monument to the man who invented neon lights," Marlowe says in *The Little Sister*. "Fifteen stories high, solid marble. There's a boy who really made something out of nothing." Marlowe's wry hopelessness is reminiscent of the "nihilists" in *The Big Lebowski*. The archetype isn't called the lonesome cowboy for nothing.

On Labor Day, James, John, and I celebrated workers' rights by spending the day at Redondo Beach. James wore his *Railroad Workers United* T-shirt, and John wore a shirt he bought at Disneyland with a picture of the villain Gaston from *Beauty and the Beast* looking in a mirror and text reading *Relationship Status? Single.* As the train conductors frolicked in the surf, I sat on the beach, taking pictures of myself with my phone and letting the sun bake me brick red. The air churned with a weird hot fog and kids dragged masses of sea plants from the water and piled them up on the sand. At one point a seagull took a shit on my shirt.

Didion, Los Angeles's great scribe, insists that the city made her see narrative as a sentimental indulgence. It's a symptom of L.A.'s disjointedness, its center that won't hold, its lack of a meaningful focal point or thesis. This is what sends Marlowe, the Dude, and Tod Hackett spinning from one corner of the city to another, alone and driftless. And this is why the detective story, which of all genres provides the audience with a concrete resolution, in Los Angeles feels ironic, anathema: the plot is "ultimately unimportant."

Watching the swimmers at Redondo Beach, I found the ocean played a trick of perspective: the hugeness of the water flattened horizontal distances, so everything—the beach and the surf and the tiny swimmers—hung vertically in the sky. The ocean also runs contrary to our desire for something comprehensive, for a solution. It is a network progressing mysteriously without a discernible center. It's massive and it's moving.

Los Angeles Diary

Lolita is a burlesque of the confessional mode, the literary
diary.

—ALFRED APPEL JR., IN HIS INTRODUCTION
TO *THE ANNOTATED LOLITA*

My first roommate in Los Angeles was offering a room
in an Echo Park bungalow/rapper crash pad. He was
an indie hip-hop producer who is in his own way pretty famous. I'd wake up to find rappers on the couch, rappers on
the living room floor, rappers in the shower or making grilled
cheese in the microwave. One night a rapper called my name
through the window when I was listening to Mariah Carey in
my room. I screamed bloody murder. He was only wondering
if I wanted to drink a beer with him on the porch.

One week my roommate and his girlfriend went to Hum-
boldt County in Northern California to camp and cut marijuana. I enjoyed having the house to myself for maybe twelve
hours, wandering around in my underwear and watching my
roommate's VHS tapes. Then J, a rapper, showed up. He had
come from San Diego to spend a week mastering his new al-

bum. J was a funny, gentle weirdo with a Kramer haircut and a tattoo of Emiliano Zapata. "In San Diego they call me EPM," he told me, "Epiphanies Per Minute." One night when J was there, my poet friend in Nebraska texted me an audio file of a poem called "Drizzy." I placed my phone on the kitchen table, and J and I gathered around it. "Why why why am I crying alone on my bed with Xbox Live home screen glow," my friend read. "I am for everyone to smile bigger than any city they fell in love with after college." J buried his head in his hands. "Let's listen to it again," he said. It was funny to see that the essence of twentysomething sorrow was no different between the stoner poets I met in the middle of nowhere and the stoner rappers I met in the middle of somewhere. This was my first indication that life in Los Angeles was odd but possible. A few days later, when my roommate came back from the wilderness, he told me that a rapper friend had just gotten into town from Chicago and he was going to stay in my room. I packed up my stuff and left on October 1.

When I drove into Hollywood for the first time that summer, I blasted "Party in the USA" by Miley Cyrus, the pop masterpiece about a girl leaving Nashville and arriving in L.A. "with a dream and my cardigan." "Look to my right, and I see the Hollywood sign," she sings, and I looked out my window, and there it was. This was exactly what pop music was invented for: to score pure moments, like a girl's first swing down the 101 onto Hollywood Boulevard. A few months later I was on a crowded city bus riding to work before dawn listening to Cyrus's album *Bangerz*, shortly after the former child star sparked a moment of mild pop culture delirium by twerking on Robin Thicke at the VMAs. "I'll show you overexposed," she seemed to say with her "Wrecking Ball" video, where she swung around naked on, yes, a wrecking ball.

The contrast here was not lost on me. But the break between Cyrus's Hannah Montana years and her new adult persona on *Bangerz* was not as stark as it appeared. To begin with, Cyrus has always been an expert at trolling her public, saying at the time that "Party in the USA" came out that she had nothing to do with the release of the song and had not even wanted it on her album. Despite what the song's chorus says—and what would seem to be nearly impossible considering her years in the music industry—she claimed in 2009 that she had never heard a Jay-Z song. And on *Bangerz* she seeks transparently to succeed her queen, Britney Spears, who even as a teen star was not that innocent.

Los Angeles was the perfect place for me to probe pop contradictions, not least because I was spending hours of my day in the car and on the bus, where, I thought wickedly, no one could even guess I was listening to ". . . Baby One More Time." That fall I wrote about new albums by Lorde and Cyrus. I wrote a love letter to Spears. Pop starlets had always been my favorites, but now they were the angels at my side, accompanying me as I made my bewildering way through the city. From drama queens like Lana Del Rey and Taylor Swift to pop machines like Rihanna and Katy Perry, I believed many of my Top 40 sisters spoke about my situation in sad, secret ways. I had no boyfriend and a terrible job and

I kept losing my wallet, so I ordered a new driver's license and then accidentally threw it in the trash, and I was sure, for some reason, that these women who had achieved unthinkable success as teenagers and were worshipped for their perfect beauty would understand. It was similar, I guess, to why people buy candles with pictures of saints on them. I wrote about pop stars in secret ways, too, taking comfort that no one would find me in the brisk music reviews I compulsively wrote.

That fall, defeated by a day of serving expensive sandwiches to television executives, I was driving on Union Street leaving downtown L.A. when I first heard "American Girl" by Bonnie McKee on a new music show on Top 40 radio. It's a juicy pop jam structured around guitar riffs brazenly ripping off "Hit Me with Your Best Shot." I later learned that it was not properly "new music" at all—it had been released in July in a bid for the title of summer anthem, reached number 87 on the Billboard Hot 100 Charts, and then fell back below the radar. The fact that the height of American patriotism coincides with the height of the summer—and the mega-success of "Party in the USA"—might explain the popular gambit of name-dropping America in your summer pop single. But what makes "American Girl" remarkable is how laced it is with pop cliché irony. McKee's vision includes the prodigious tackiness of the United States. "I fell in love in a 7-Eleven parking lot," the song begins. She gets only more biting about our national character, as in the best line in the track's chorus: "I was raised by a television. / Every day is a competition." The picture she paints of an American girl is someone ambitious, independent, rebellious, and trashy.

The "American Girl" music video is even cheekier and more frenetic than the song: McKee and her gang of white girls do porny dances in a 7-Eleven and in front of a vending machine. They play the retro board game Girl Talk and hang out at the mall. McKee chills by a pool wearing American-flag-print Lolita sunglasses. They drive a red Mustang to In-N-Out, then out past the Hollywood Sign to the canyons surrounding Los Angeles. At the end, the Mustang inexplicably explodes into flames, so McKee and her friends roast marshmallows. McKee illustrates Los Angeles's special boredom—there is nothing to do, but so much trouble to get into. She's not the only one who has believed the essential invocation of the American (and more specifically Californian) spirit is the bored, sexually mature suburban teenager.

My second roommate in Los Angeles, K, was a twenty-one-year-old who had a cat named after Joan Didion. That was the main reason I moved in with her. She was offering a two-month sublet in her apartment on the far western edge of Echo Park. She had gotten the apartment with her best friend, who never moved in. The complex raked up from the crowded street in a series of rose-filled terraces. K showed me sheepishly how the place seemed to be made out of Styrofoam and cardboard. "I got drunk, fell down, and kicked a hole in the wall," she said, pointing out an opening in the thin plaster. The first night I moved in, ants came out from cracks in the closet and swarmed my backpack. She gave me

Lysol, which I sprayed over the entire surface of the floor and on many of my belongings. I had no furniture. A few days after I moved in, the bulb in the overhead light burned out. K told me hers had stopped working months before, and she had been using candles ever since. I was at my waitressing job seven miles away in Century City from ten A.M. to nine P.M. most days, and when I got home, I watched *Dateline* and ate hot-sauce-flavored potato chips by the light of my laptop. I slept on the floor the whole time I lived there.

"Something bad happened to me today," K said one night when I came home. She had put a bottle of white wine in the freezer and forgotten about it, and it exploded. She carefully hoarded the hunks of frozen wine in my Tupperware.

"Aren't you afraid of drinking glass?" I said.

"I made an Indiegogo page to fund a new bottle of wine," she said.

Three weeks in, she told me that her best friend wanted to move in after all, and I would have to move out after one month instead of two. My clothes and books were still in the milk crates I had moved them in.

My third roommate in Los Angeles was an actor in his forties, V. His apartment was in a strange old row house in the heart of Koreatown. "Okay, I'm just going to be honest with you," he said the first time I met him. He told me the landlords were elderly and apparently insane. He had convinced them that his friend who had lived in the apartment for fifteen years had never moved out, so that he could maintain rent control. "If you lived here, you would have to pretend to be my girlfriend," he said. "And the hot water doesn't work in the kitchen." I moved in five days later.

A few weeks after I moved in, I passed V in the kitchen.

"I forgot to tell you. There's a homeless man named Gary who lives in our carport. I give him five dollars a week," he told me. "The landlords know about him," he added to ease my mind.

I continued boiling spaghetti in my hot pot.

"Gary might call you 'you guys,' even though there's only one of you," he said. "He hasn't been looking good. I don't think he'll live much longer."

Halfway through Lana Del Rey's *Paradise* EP, she breaks out a lugubrious cover of the standard "Blue Velvet," and no one is surprised. She has always shared filmmaker David Lynch's fetish for fifties and sixties culture, singing about looking for her James Dean and the "fifties baby doll dress" she would wear to her wedding. With Lynch's twisted fifties aesthetic as a guiding standard, Del Rey's music is an innovative mix of trip hop and cabaret, featuring both echoey drum beats and cinematic strings, sometimes stripped down, fuzzy, washed out, other times lush and retro. She has developed a fully imagined persona that goes way beyond the concept album, something like a freaky Connie Francis with a death wish.

In the United States, the 1950s are idealized as the most wholesomely American decade, riding the pride of winning World War II into the paranoid patriotism of the Cold War. Precisely because of this wholesomeness, fifties America is a trope that is easily, and enjoyably, perverted. This era is where white America places a lot of its nostalgia when it longs to be great again—*Leave It to Beaver* helps efface the Montgomery Bus Boycott, just as it was designed to. Del Rey's music is overtly about America, with song titles like "American" and "National Anthem." She is obsessed with her cultural origins—who begot her, who formed her vision of herself. Maybe this is why she displays a self-consciously Freudian interest in fucking her dad. Most of the relationships she describes have a creepy daddy-daughter dynamic. Most stunning are two lines from her song "Cola": "I fall asleep with an American flag . . . / I pledge allegiance to my dad."

"Light of my life, fire in my loins, / Be a good baby, do what I want," Del Rey sings on "Off to the Races." *Lolita* is a twisted vision of fifties America, too, a charming road novel about a pedophile and his kidnapped stepdaughter. *Lolita*'s power is in how it demonstrates the lure of evil and the banality of innocence, with its slick, seductive narrator, Humbert Humbert, and his repulsively ordinary victim, Dolores. Humbert's attractiveness cannot be separated from his European identity, and Dolores's crassness can't be separated from her American one. If the American spirit is a bored, sexually mature suburban teenager, then Del Rey does everything she can to embody her.

"Is 'mask' the keyword?" Humbert Humbert asks in *Lolita*. Alfred Appel Jr., tireless annotator of *Lolita*, directs us to a moment where Humbert's narrative mask slips. In the novel's shortest chapter, we get a vision of Humbert in jail, despairing, "Have written more than a hundred pages and not got anywhere yet." Nabokov famously inserted himself in *Lolita* by using anagrams of his own name, most notably Vivian Darkbloom. Del Rey hides in plain sight, too, but sometimes it's not clear whether her Lolita burlesque is actually the disguise. "Like a groupie incognito posing as a real singer," she sings, "life imitates art." Is *mask* the keyword? It's a feat to make yourself disappear while actually being straightforward, honest, even autobiographical.

In a 1967 interview with *The Paris Review*, Vladimir Nabokov said:

> Another project I have been nursing for some time is the publication of the complete screenplay of *Lolita* that I made for Kubrick [. . .] The film is only a blurred skimpy glimpse of the marvelous picture I imagined and set down scene by scene during the six months I worked in a Los Angeles villa. I do not wish to imply that Kubrick's film is mediocre; in its own right, it is first-rate, but it is not what I wrote. A tinge of poshlost is often given by the cinema to the novel it distorts and coarsens in its crooked glass.

This strikes me as a very Los Angeles story. Los Angeles is a land of iterations, versions of versions, a swimming pool's endless refractions, a city that sprawls forever. "Oh, my Lolita, I have only words to play with!" Humbert says. Is it obvious I don't know what I'm doing here? I have no sense of Los Angeles. With this diary I build a collection of things I have authority to speak on. Light of my Lana, fire of my Lana. My song, my sort of.

Things with V were good, except for the several months that we had to pet-sit a hairless cat for his ex-girlfriend—in fact, the woman who had sublet me her room. The cat was always plotting ways to get into my room, thinking it was his, and I was unable to get him out if he ever tricked his way in, since I didn't want to touch his furless skin. Gary died in the spring.

One day when I was home, someone shoved a piece of paper between the front door and its frame saying the land-lords would be at the apartment later that week. Our neighbor's apartment was sinking, V told me flatly, and our place was at risk of being condemned by the city, forcing the landlords to visit their neglected property. Having never put our relation-ship ruse into practice, I wasn't sure how I was supposed to act and was terrified of accidentally revealing our fraud. As I left for work on Friday, I came face-to-face with an ancient man with charcoal hair oiled back like Jimmy Stewart's. He looked at me with obscure suspicion, but he didn't say any-thing.

Lonely Heart

A few years ago my friend Paul posted on Twitter: "when you finally 'get' the britney spears song HIT ME BABY ONE MORE TIME like 15 years after hearing it for the first time." This had been on my mind, too: how ". . . Baby One More Time" had started to strike me as very deep and very sad. Spears's first single is comfortably one of the most important pop songs of all time. The song and its iconic music video, featuring sixteen-year-old Spears in a Catholic school uniform dancing provocatively through a high school's hallways, rang in the teen pop craze of the late nineties and early aughts, when a generation of Spears's fellow former Disney Channel stars busted out of Orlando and went (a little) wild.

I think most people grant that ". . . Baby One More Time" is a good song. Its production is visceral: the opening piano chords that summon pop spirits, the wah-wah guitars, the cymbal crashes, and the use of background vocals are all distinctive. And this was the first showcase for Spears's singing voice, which is sexy, abrasive, and strange. ". . . Baby One More Time" has all the features of an incredible late-era pop single: simple hooks over tightly layered production, designed to move your mood, not your mind.

Why is it anything more than that? Spears has had two dozen major hits since ". . . Baby One More Time" was released in 1998, and her singles "Stronger," "Oops! . . . I Did It Again," and "(You Drive Me) Crazy" are all remarkably similar to ". . . Baby One More Time" in their composition. Still, her first song remains her greatest hit. ". . . Baby One More Time" doesn't just tower over her other singles because it was the first, or because she tied up her school uniform shirt in the music video. Paul tweeted:

> *my loneliness*
> *is killing me.*
>
> *—britney spears*

She sings this over and over: So why had I never heard it?

". . . Baby One More Time" is a product of the music industry's bubblegum factory if there ever was one. Shortly after Spears signed with Jive Records, she flew to Stockholm to work with Swedish producers. Joyful, creative, insidiously catchy pop music has long been one of Sweden's top exports, and its stars like ABBA, Ace of Base, and Robyn along with its super producers like Dr. Luke and Stargate all bow to Swedish pop god Max Martin.

Producer and songwriter Martin wrote or cowrote seventeen number one hits in fifteen years, including the Backstreet

Boys' "I Want It That Way," NSYNC's "It's Gonna Be Me," Kelly Clarkson's "Since U Been Gone," Taylor Swift's "We Are Never Ever Getting Back Together," and Katy Perry's "Roar." Martin first met Spears in 1998 when he played her the demo for "Hit Me Baby One More Time." TLC passed on the song, but Spears and her team instantly saw that the track was, as a Jive A&R executive put it, "a fucking smash."

". . . Baby One More Time" is so entwined with Spears's persona that it seems bizarre that it wasn't written for her. How could any other artist have sung it? But then again, of course they could have. Pop songwriters are necessarily mercenary, offering their services to the artist who will take them. And the song's connection to TLC is an interesting one. Spears's emergence signaled a sea change in popular music, away from the funky R&B of the mid-1990s, exemplified by TLC and Janet Jackson, toward a sound that was younger, whiter, and on the surface, more sexually innocent. Spears's record label tried to tone down ". . . Baby One More Time" by removing the "hit me" from the title, but the song is still knowing in a way that's closer to *CrazySexyCool* than "As Long As You Love Me." Like any good opportunist, Martin found a way to turn the old thing into the next big thing.

I was an actual Catholic schoolgirl at the age of sixteen, and it was so dismally far from the music video fantasy. The Catholic high school I went to for a semester in Nebraska was underfunded and strange. At the end of the school year we had to hot-glue our textbooks back together. From what

I could tell, the school's prime objective was to instruct students not to have abortions or vote for John Kerry.

I jumped ship the first week of my senior year. I decided to get my GED, which if you've been to a majority of high school is, as my GED counselor told me, "a mute point." But because I was under eighteen, regulations put forth by the state of Nebraska to dissuade people from dropping out of high school dictated that I had to take ten hours of GED training at the local community college. I finished all of the preparatory materials before my ten hours were up, so the teacher running the training sessions let me put my head down on my desk.

In the same obstructive spirit as the required training hours, I was told I could not actually receive my GED certificate until I was eighteen. However, they did give me a letter that served as notice that I had passed the exam. At sixteen, I sent the University of Nebraska my GED letter and an essay I wrote about a book I hadn't read, and they let me into the honors program.

The most prominent part of Spears's personal brand has always been that she is *like* a virgin, vacillating absolutely inconsistently between performing as an adolescent girl and as a sexually mature woman. Part of her "little girl" act is pretending not to understand the sexual attention she elicits. "All I did was tie up my shirt!" she told *Rolling Stone* in 1999 about the ". . . Baby One More Time" video. "I'm wearing a sports bra under it. Sure, I'm wearing thigh-highs, but kids wear those—it's the style. Have you seen MTV—all those in thongs?"

And yet Spears has been remarkably self-aware—even calculating—about the conflicts in her persona. Her hit "I'm Not a Girl, Not Yet a Woman," from her coming-of-age movie *Crossroads*, is the most blatant expression of this trope, or maybe it's the "Oops! . . . I Did It Again" video, where eighteen-year-old Spears dances in a skintight red vinyl bodysuit and sings, "I'm not that innocent."

There is no doubt that her personal contradictions are heightened by the brilliant, dissonant images in her music videos. People have credited the ". . . Baby One More Time" video with all of the song's success, a sixteen-year-old brashly seizing on a naughty schoolgirl porno fantasy and immediately positioning herself at the center of the national imagination. "Is Spears bubblegum jailbait, jaded crossover diva or malleable Stepford teen?" *Rolling Stone* asked in 1999. "Who knows? Whether by design or not, the queen of America's new Teen Age is a distinctly modern anomaly: the anonymous superstar."

In "Overprotected," released ten days after Spears's twentieth birthday, she makes several startling complaints. "I tell them what I like, what I want, what I don't," she sings. "But every time I do, I stand corrected." She's singing not as a post-adolescent coming into her own, but as a woman who has been guarded and controlled by handlers since she was fifteen. She is self-aware in performing not only the naughty schoolgirl but also the anonymous superstar, her body a projection screen that all of the world's desires can flicker across.

Her early hit "Lucky" is an unsubtle allegory about a starlet named Lucky who dreams of escaping fame. How perverse that Martin would write this song for Spears, and her managers would agree that she should record it, then release it as a single and profit off it. "She's so lucky," Spears sings, "she's a star / But she cry, cry, cries in her lonely heart." When we confront it, this sadness is so much more dissonant than the sex in her videos. *My loneliness. Is killing me. My loneliness. Is killing me.*

A little while later, Paul texted me, "do you ever feel that your level of intelligence dooms you to be alone." My reply began, "My answer is I think sort of obviously yes." My intelligence setting me apart is a lie that has driven my life in ways I'm only beginning to interrogate. When I tell people I went to college at sixteen, they get a vision of a super-special whiz kid that I'm happy to indulge. When I think about my college experience, what I see is not overachiever syndrome but an almost sociopathic delight in being ahead, in tricking the system. This shows a kind of intelligence, but not necessarily that of the wunderkind I've pretended to be.

I did not really pay attention or learn anything in college. Many weeks I skipped more classes than I went to. I spent four years alone in the dark of my parents' house eating canned ravioli and watching MTV. I manipulated and bullshitted my way to a bachelor's degree at the age of nineteen, and I knew exactly what I was doing. But when I think about my classmates who went to class and read the books, whom I felt so much distance from, it's obvious the joke was on me.

That's why sixteen-year-old Britney Spears has started to fill me with such pathos—she knew exactly what she was do-

ing, too, though I'm not saying it was the same thing I did.
I was very lonely in college. I knew I was different from the
people surrounding me, but it wasn't because I was smarter
than they were. It goes back to the reason I wanted to go to
college at sixteen at all, a decision that from the beginning
guaranteed only that I would never have a dorm-rooms-and-
keg-parties college experience. I got too good at isolating myself, which was not intelligence but more likely the clichéd
coexistence of self-hatred and self-obsession.

Is pop music smart?

It is easy to attribute the brilliance of ". . . Baby One More
Time" to the familiar accident where a whole is greater than
the sum of its parts. We can draw up a diagram of the con-
tributing factors for its success: Max Martin, Jive Records,
trends in Top 40 radio, Debbie Gibson, Monica Lewinsky,
the Disney Channel, and, very last, Spears herself. It goes
back to capitalism's odd vision of "the market," which knows
everything but is not intelligent by the same standard we
would judge life on other planets.

But to my mind, ". . . Baby One More Time" speaks as
keenly about the loneliness of love as any other artifact of our
culture: it's not about losing someone but the impossibility of
ever really having them. "When I'm not with you, I lose my
mind," Spears sings. Romantic love doesn't lessen the opacity
of other people's thoughts and motivations. It heightens it,
because the desire to know and inhabit the beloved's mind
is so great. That's what makes us sick in love, crazy in love.
Short experiences of union reinforce that each of us is, once

and for all, a single person, alone in a body, known only to the self.

I'm not reading too much into the song. Pop music can speak deep truths because it is simple, because the truest truths are simple. What isn't simple is a sixteen-year-old in her expected setting—a high school—singing about grown-up desperation. Or an artist whose greatest creative preoccupation seems to be a smiling sadomasochism—"hit me baby" and vinyl bodysuits, the giant snake on her shoulders as she sang "I'm a Slave 4 U"—being labeled as "America's Sweetheart." Or a woman hunted by paparazzi who photographed her working out, going to Starbucks, driving recklessly with her son on her lap, shaving her head; who photographed her genitals as she got out of her limo for an audience that loved her almost to death.

"I guess I can't see the harm in working and being a mama," Spears sang in 2007, just after her series of personal crises, with her signature false naïveté. Britney Spears's music is about desire; from the beginning, Britney Spears herself has been about a prodigious contradiction, a prodigious loneliness. Watch the end of the ". . . Baby One More Time" video, as Spears holds her face with boredom and smirks at the camera, her pigtail braids secured with feather scrunchies, and witness the spark: it's not the dumb hand of the market patting her head with approval, nor sex and its dumb compulsions, nor even the dumb intelligence that is satire or critique. It's that other thing. Art.

The Place Makes
Everyone a Gambler

When I first moved to Los Angeles, I sat by Echo Park Lake and read Joan Didion's 1970 novel *Play It As It Lays* twice. You have to be a special kind of depressive to read this book more than once, especially more than once back to back. It follows Maria Wyeth, actress and model of minimal success and wife to an up-and-coming movie director, as her life falls apart. Her young daughter, Kate, suffers from a mysterious mental disability and is institutionalized. Maria files for divorce. She gets an abortion. She becomes, in her agent's words, "a slightly suicidal situation."

Although *Play It As It Lays* has achieved classic status—it was on *Time*'s list of the 100 best English-language novels since 1923—many readers find Maria unbearably dramatic, self-centered, messy, and babyish. It takes a personality with both a tendency toward old-fashioned melodrama and a ruthless, sad/beautiful, cinematic nihilism to pick up what

Play It As It Lays is putting down—which is maybe to say it takes a bad personality.

I sat on a crumbling stone bench set into the greenery surrounding the lake, and dead bird-of-paradise flowers got tangled in my hair. It was lovely: ducks hung out in the shallows and the statue of the Lady of the Lake laid her shadow in the water. But as I observed the men pushing ice cream carts, the families, dogs, and joggers circling the lake, it was as if everything I saw concealed a dark edge, a poison that floated imperceptibly in the daylight. Toddlers almost pitched themselves into the water when their parents looked away. A man threw a tennis ball into the lake and his little dog swam out to retrieve it over and over again. Every time it looked to me like the dog would falter, she had gotten too tired, she might drown right there near the fountain.

At one point in *Play It As It Lays* Maria takes in the action in the town square of a small beach town. She watches "some boys in ragged Levi jackets and dark goggles . . . passing a joint with furtive daring" and "an old man [who] coughed soundlessly, spit phlegm that seemed to hang in the heavy air." Maria fantasizes about calling her lover and, in making contact, undoing her dread. "Maybe she would hear his voice and the silence would break," Didion writes, "the woman in the nurse's uniform would speak to her charge and the boys would get on their Harleys and roar off."

Maria's anxiety is evidence of the secret patterns, connections, and implications that a mind accrues when it talks only to itself. "Her mind was a blank tape," Didion writes of Maria, "imprinted daily with snatches of things overheard . . .

the beginnings of jokes and odd lines of song lyrics." Her life becomes inseparable from her dreams: images and figures and words and sounds collected, recombined, and imbued with sinister meaning.

Throughout *Play It As It Lays*, Maria dreams of her dead mother, a shadowy "syndicate" hiding bodies in the plumbing of her house, fetuses floating in the East River, and children filing into a gas chamber. Waking and dreaming, she is preoccupied with rattlesnakes, and her pregnancy and the aftermath of her abortion are dark and strange as a nightmare. Shortly after I moved into my first sublet in Los Angeles, I opened my laptop in the morning and tiny grease ants started crawling out of the cracks in the keyboard. I'd never encountered grease ants, which are so small that they crawled in under the cap of my closed jar of peanut butter, forming what I at first mistook for a film of dust. Sometimes dream symbolism collides with waking life by coincidence, but sometimes it is a bad sign, maybe indicating that I had ended up where I didn't—or couldn't—belong, not equipped financially for the city, and not equipped emotionally for the only life I could afford. Dread was, as it always is, an explanation, a sidelong look at what I couldn't control.

Didion's experimentation with dream structure in *Play It As It Lays* may have something to do with her suspicion of the unity, linearity, and cause and effect of traditional narrative. Didion is one of the essential essayists of the twentieth century, and all great nonfiction writers examine how the coherence we expect from storytelling is incompatible with the contradictions and competing truths of real life. I think of Janet Malcolm, who over her twelve books has considered the way narrative is created in psychology, journalism, and biography: the artificial order each lays over real life. Malcolm writes in *The Journalist and the Murderer*:

> As every work of fiction draws on life, so every work of nonfiction draws on art. As the novelist must curb his imagination in order to keep his text grounded in the common experience of man (dreams exemplify the uncurbed imagination— thus their uninterestingness to everyone but their author), so the journalist must temper his literal-mindedness with the narrative devices of imaginative literature.

In this way, Didion walks a careful line in *Play It As It Lays*. She can't avoid all the traditional conventions of the novel form, and she can't ignore the mandates of fact. But she must find a way to shape a novel that reflects that archipelago of an industry that is "entertainment," and Los Angeles, a city whose unifying characteristic is its disjointedness.

Play It As It Lays begins with Maria compulsively and aimlessly driving L.A.'s freeway system. "She drove it as a riverman runs a river," Didion writes, and when Maria is not driving, she fantasizes about it, replaying in her mind perfectly merging from one freeway to another with a balletic shift across four lanes of traffic. This practice indicates Maria's absolute idleness—her husband and daughter have both been taken away from her, so she has nothing to occupy her time or her thoughts. But she is also seeking emptiness. Driving can be a meditative activity, the mind and the body working in unison, moving in response to stimuli—the road, the lane, the signs and signals, the other drivers—without conscious thought: the flow of the fugitive act. "Sometimes at night the dread would overtake her," Didion writes, "bathe her in sweat, flood her mind with sharp flash images . . . but she never thought about that on the freeway."

Driving L.A. is one of Didion's favorite themes in her nonfiction, too: in 1976 she described driving the city as requiring "total surrender, a concentration so intense as to seem a kind of narcosis, a rapture-of-the-freeway." In 1989 she wrote how these hours spent in one's car effect "a kind of seductive unconnectedness" in which

> context clues are missing. In Culver City as in Echo Park as in East Los Angeles, there are the same pastel bungalows. There are the same leggy poinsettia and the same trees of pink and yellow hibiscus.

"Rapture-of-the-freeway" is maybe writing it a bit too large. For me, driving in L.A. was not a narcotic but the most terrifying kind of stimulant. I always felt like I was risking death, my own and that of unfortunate Los Angeles pedestrians who appeared as scary aberrations in the landscape, wandering around the Rite Aid parking lot or running across Normandie to the Laundromat. I spent much more time riding the bus and walking (risking death by a different method) than anyone I knew. I saw accidents all the time: cars spin-ning out on the freeway on sunny days; Lexuses backing up into other Lexuses in the parking lot at my job; a guy jump-ing the gun at a green light north of my place in Koreatown and ramming into the bumper in front of him, then both drivers getting out to yell at and threaten each other. At the same time, driving in Los Angeles is freeing in the way that all disasters are. Where I previously followed my driver's ed teacher's maxim that you must see a car's tires in your rear-view mirror before merging in front of it, I learned to look over my shoulder and quickly wedge myself into any car-sized space that had appeared in traffic.

In this, I understand the contradiction of experience—enforced lawlessness, trapped freedom, humdrum danger—that Didion is getting at in *Play It As It Lays*: freeway driving, navigating the network of loops and interchanges that take you right back where you started from, is uniquely appropriate for Maria's erratic, desperate kind of heroine. If the open road is an American totem of independence and escape, what does it mean when the road is actually a closed circuit? In Vanessa Grigoriadis's infamous 2008 *Rolling Stone* profile of Britney Spears, "The Tragedy of Britney Spears," she writes about the routine Spears made of paparazzi chases: "She races around [Los Angeles] for two or three hours a day, aimlessly leading paps to various locations where she could interact with them just a little bit and then jump back into her car."

Grigoriadis surveys Spears's struggles from 2003 to 2008, "the most public downfall of any star in history," as she descended from America's golden pop star through quickie marriages, rehab stays, her children being legally removed from her custody, and one very public head-shaving incident to rock bottom. Grigoriadis describes her as "an inbred swamp thing who chain-smokes, doesn't do her nails, tells reporters to 'eat it, snort it, lick it, fuck it' and screams at people who want pictures for their little sisters." "The Tragedy of Britney Spears" is pure exploitive Hollywood camp, a lurid and gossipy rundown of sad events that were already public property. The strange thing about Didion's Hollywood novel is that this sort of pulp journalism is where we are used to encountering characters like Maria, not in meditations on existential nothingness.

Grigoriadis admits, "it may be true that Britney suffers from the adult onset of a genetic mental disorder . . . or that she is a 'habitual, frequent and continuous' drug user," but she does not deem these explanations of the Britney Spears "tragedy" worthy of exploration. They would hazard too much empathy, rendering Spears a human to connect with, rather than a spectacle to gawk at. But as Grigoriadis describes Spears's unpredictable driving—"a Britney chase is more fun than a roller coaster"—I'm struck by the bizarre sadness of the situation, a young woman fleeing an army of mysterious men for hours every day, driving away just to find herself driving back, always being caught, rooted out. It's like a bad dream.

The insanity of Los Angeles's epically unsustainable urban development is that it was all on purpose, the dizzying system of freeways uniquely supporting the vision of the real estate barons who created the city. Didion writes: "This would be a new kind of city, one that would seem to have no finite limits, a literal cloud on the land." This is why certain attributes that seem accidental, "the sprawl of the city, the apparent absence of a cohesive center," are in fact imperative to Los Angeles's raison d'être and are why driving is "for many people who live in Los Angeles, the dead center of being there." The idealism of this "cloud on the land" stands in ironic juxtaposition to many facts about Los Angeles, like its constant, looming natural disasters, including wildfires, mudslides, and earthquakes. But one thrust of Didion's project is probing the ways that the threat of disaster is not opposed to the Los Angeles dream of endless sprawl. In the idealists' eyes, the Los Angeles of today or yesterday is impermanent, indeterminate, and unimportant. It can always be torn down, rebuilt, and reimagined. I'm collecting examples of a certain L.A. yin-yang: disaster and development, "The Tragedy of Britney Spears" and *Play It As It Lays*, film language and dream language.

In my first sublet in Echo Park, when I could pick up my neighbors' Wi-Fi, I obsessively watched the true crime documentary series *Dateline NBC* on YouTube, particularly those episodes hosted by Keith Morrison, a rakish, ghoulish Canadian journalist with a luxurious mane of white hair, who seems to take macabre pleasure in the stories of people killing their spouses for insurance money, killing their lovers' spouses, pushing their business partners off boats, or bludgeoning strangers while on meth benders. Obviously I took pleasure in it, too. The show is at once depressing and filled with weird comedy, like the time the show's voice-over said about a victim, "Her new man made her tingle as if ginger ale had filled her heart." This seemed suited to the dark comedy of my own life as I lay on the floor of my bedless sublet, eating junk food.

Many episodes of *Dateline* take place in Los Angeles's outlying areas, suburbs and small towns in Orange County or San Bernardino County or the Antelope Valley, places where residents might think they are sheltered, just beyond the reach of urban chaos. These are mostly towns developed in the mid-twentieth century, part of that tract-house-studded Sunbelt that saw a huge growth in population with the Cold War aerospace boom. People migrated for the chance to re-invent themselves as members of the all-American middle class in shiny Southern California, a chance to lead lives like the families they saw on television. And for some, that dream was realized: for many of the interviewees on *Dateline*, it seems like they can't believe their lives have become TV-worthy. Murder is the only interesting thing that has ever happened to them.

The *Dateline* mysteries about these boom suburbs are a peculiar bait and switch. These people came to California to become producers, but they became part of the product, and not even the most important part. The victims and their families are given due screen time on *Dateline*, but it is mostly generic, perfunctory. "She could make a whole room smile," a family member says about one victim. "He loved being a dad," we hear about another. The best parts of any *Dateline* episode are about the murderer and the police's process of tracking him or her down, because the feelings are more straightforward: there's nothing to complicate the audience's basically clinical fascination with violent crime and detective work. "This is the story of a mother," Morrison might say to introduce a victim, but the story is elsewhere.

Our cultural obsession with murder stories and the criminal justice system is a prime example of the impulse to narrativize a reality that is basically unexplainable. For better or worse, narrative is the tool that the system uses to deliver justice: the defense and the prosecution each present their stories, and the one that makes more sense—read as: the more satisfying one—becomes the reality. Didion writes in her 1989 essay "L.A. Noir" about a murder case that generated significant media attention because of the peripheral involvement of the onetime head of production of Paramount Pictures, Robert Evans, and a movie he was planning to produce, *The Cotton Club*. Although the case's connection to Evans and his movie were dubious, every movie, book, and piece proposed about it involved Evans, so that the shorthand for the case became "Cotton Club," inevitably implying Evans's guilt. For both the media covering a case and the district attorney, a murder is a story to be sold, whether to a movie studio, a publishing house, or a jury. For Didion, the Cotton Club case affirms the Hollywood faith "in killings, both literal and figurative":

> In fact this kind of faith is not unusual in Los Angeles. In a city not only largely conceived as a series of real estate promotions but largely supported by a series of confidence games, a city even then afloat

on motion pictures and junk bonds and the B-2 Stealth bomber, the conviction that something can be made of nothing may be one of the few narratives in which everyone participates.

This idea of Los Angeles's massive communal roll of the dice is essential to Didion's understanding of the city, that cloud on the land, and especially the entertainment industry. "The place makes everyone a gambler," she writes. "Its spirit is speedy, obsessive, immaterial." She describes how a project's financing—the phrases "the deal" or "the action" are how Didion writes about the business of bankrolling movies—is the true story of any movie, and it's over before production even begins. An excellent case study in the deal is Stephen Rodrick's January 2013 *New York Times Magazine* feature "The Misfits." It chronicles the making of Paul Schrader and Bret Easton Ellis's microbudget sex thriller *The Canyons*, which stars Lindsay Lohan and porn star James Deen. Schrader, writer of the classic films *Raging Bull* and *Taxi Driver*, and Bret Easton Ellis, iconic enfant terrible novelist of *American Psycho* fame, were both dangerously close to washed up and looking to make something of nothing, to regenerate both of their careers with one sensational project.

Just how they intended to do that is the subject of Rodrick's article. Schrader wanted to "do something on the cheap that didn't look cheap." There is extensive speculation about where the money is. Schrader and his partners design a deal in which *The Canyons* would be "the most open film ever," with an interactive social media presence and a "populist" approach to financing, using the crowdfunding platform Kickstarter, with "no studio looking over their shoulders offering idiot notes." They cast Deen and Lohan, an infamously troubled former child star, to gain publicity for the project. This, the evolving financial deal of *The Canyons*, is the story of "The Misfits," as much as it pretends to be about the on-set chaos caused by Lohan.

Lohan's melodramatics serve as an object lesson in the difficulties of trying to make a movie in an unconventional way. One day when the crew is filming in a Santa Monica shopping mall, she sees a magazine with Oliver Stone on the cover and rips it up, cursing him for refusing to cast her in a movie. When this piece made a stir among the people I followed on social media, a few months before I moved to California, I thought of Grigoriadis's piece on Spears immediately, and about the camp film disaster-piece *Valley of the Dolls*, which depicts the fresh-faced and wholesome Patty Duke transforming into a showbiz banshee, manically gobbling uppers and downers. These, and *Play It As It Lays*, too, were part of an L.A. syllabus I made for myself before I even knew I would live there. It illustrated how big questions about the mechanics of the city and the entertainment industry— who was in charge and who profited—could be obliquely probed or sidestepped altogether by focusing on the messy theatrics of washed-up white women. Grigoriadis describes a tantrum in which Spears's credit card is declined. "A wail emerges . . . guttural, vile, the kind of base animalistic shriek only heard at a family member's deathbed," she writes, really going for the gusto. "'Fuck these bitches,' screams Britney, each word ringing out between sobs. 'These idiots can't do anything right!'"

In her nonfiction, Didion resists the popular narrative of the entertainment industry's sordidness, insisting of young Hollywood in the seventies that "the average daily narcotic intake is one glass of a three-dollar Mondavi white and two marijuana cigarettes shared by six people." But *Play It As It Lays* seems to send a different message: there is plenty of the degeneracy we expect from pictures of Hollywood excess, like the sex life of Maria and Carter's friends Helene and BZ, who indulge in swinging, group sex, S&M, and voyeurism. Like Rodrick's article, but at a more fundamental level, *Play It As It Lays* is about the deal: Didion contemplates the existential gamble we undertake in our daily struggles, as we all strive, in the end, toward nothing but nothingness. And like in Grigoriadis's article, it is very easy to become distracted by the woman at the novel's center: Maria's clothes, her jet-setting, her lounging by the pool, and her self-destruction that can seem like just one more indulgence. Lohan and Spears and Maria are all being used to sell a story—just like *Dateline* uses the smiling faces of its victims—and they are selling a story about the way we sell ourselves stories. That's what I didn't understand before I moved to L.A.: that the killings both literal and figurative did not just coexist but depended on each other, that what most people profit off of is human pain, and here I am, selling my own.

If an analogue for *Play It As It Lays* can be found in Didion's nonfiction, it is her classic essay "The White Album," in which Didion, describing a personal experience of failing mental health in the late sixties, decides that her own associative break might actually have been an appropriate response to societal stimuli. She quotes from her own psychiatric report:

> It is as though she feels deeply that all human effort is foredoomed to failure, a conviction which seems to push her further into a dependent, passive withdrawal. In her view she lives in a world of people moved by strange, conflicted, poorly comprehended, and, above all, devious motivations which commit them inevitably to conflict and failure.

In this state of withdrawal, she recalls experiences "devoid of any logic save that of the dreamwork."

As with Maria's "blank tape" mind, imprinted with sensory detritus, so Didion writes, "All I knew was what I saw: flash pictures in variable sequence, images with no 'meaning' beyond their temporary arrangement, not a movie but a cutting-room experience." No plot or narrative, just a jumble of strange, conflicted, poorly comprehended images that, when viewed in montage, say nothing.

Didion was preoccupied during this period with high-profile Hollywood murders, especially the killings committed by Charles Manson and his followers. It seems that murder stories inspire Didion with a special dread: attempting to lay thematic order over dumb chaos and cruelty starkly and distastefully reveals the cheapness of narrative. Didion asks Linda Kasabian, star witness for the prosecution in the

Manson trial, about the events that led to her involvement with the Manson Family and their monstrous crime spree that left six people dead: "Everything was to teach me something," Kasabian replied. This sort of odd and oddly self-centered conclusion is all that can be created out of so much destruction.

"The White Album" meditates on a haunting "house blessing" that hung in Didion's mother-in-law's house: it concluded, "And bless each door that opens wide, to stranger as to kin." The verse "had on [Didion] the effect of a physical chill" because it seemed like "the kind of 'ironic' detail" that appears in murder stories. In Didion's imaginative dread, it was ironic and at the same time fitting that a proclamation of goodwill and trust toward outsiders might preside over the violent betrayal of that trust. This is certainly the kind of detail that episodes of *Dateline* hang on. Didion at the time lived in a decaying mansion in an increasingly dangerous area of Hollywood. It had become what one of Didion's acquaintances called "a senseless killing neighborhood," where they did not bless the door that opened wide.

Didion and her family were renting the mansion only until zoning changes allowed its owners to tear it down and build high-rise apartments. "It was precisely this anticipation," Didion writes, "of imminent but not exactly immediate destruction that lent the neighborhood its particular character." This anticipation is the truth of Los Angeles existence writ small, that tenuousness stemming from the city's endless development and apocalyptic weather. But of course, ultimate destruction is also the only real truth of capital-E Existence.

What strikes me in Didion's craft is not only her ethical grappling with narrative but the technical difficulty of making stories out of characters like Maria who are so solitary. When I think of the loneliest time of my life, it is a queasy loop recording. In my early days in Los Angeles, I did the same things over and over again—walked to the lake, rode the bus, lost my wallet, bought a coconut ice pop—and everything seemed connected, because nothing was. There was no story, because there were no other people.

The other notable locus of raw material for *Play It As It Lays* in Didion's nonfiction is her 1965 essay "On Morality," in which she searches for a useful definition of morality in a motel room in Death Valley. Didion describes a car accident on the highway between Las Vegas and Death Valley in which a young man was killed and his girlfriend was seriously injured. Didion speaks to the nurse who drove the young woman 185 miles to the nearest doctor, and whose husband kept watch over the young man's body all night. "You can't just leave a body on the highway," the nurse says. "It's immoral." Didion respects this definition of morality because its application is precise: "She meant that if a body is left alone for even a few minutes on the desert," Didion writes, "the coyotes close in and eat the flesh." In *Play It As It Lays*, Maria's mother dies in a car accident in the desert, and the coyotes get to her first.

The action in *Play It As It Lays* moves very intentionally from the city to the desert: a cleansed landscape that is dangerous, absent, and elemental. Maria grew up in the desert, in a settlement called Silver Wells that her father, a true western prospector, developed to capitalize on the traffic from a highway that was never built. Silver Wells became a ghost town; both Maria's mother and her home are subsumed by the desert. This helps explain Maria's infatuation with nothingness. In the beginning of the novel, when she is being analyzed in a psychiatric hospital, she writes "NOTHING APPLIES" in response to her doctors' questions. "What does apply, they ask later," Maria says, "as if the word 'nothing' were ambiguous." Toward the end of the novel, "nothing" looms with mystical importance. "Tell me what matters," BZ asks her. "Nothing," Maria replies. "Tell me what you want," Carter says to her. "Nothing," Maria replies.

This nihilism seems to contradict the gambler's optimism Maria learned from her father, who raised her to believe "that what came in on the next roll would always be better than what went out on the last." For Maria and her companions, the desert strips life down to its most basic meaning: that is, no meaning. This is why Maria allows BZ to commit suicide, a decision that forms the climax of the novel. He desired nothingness, and he reached out for it. What could be more natural? But if the answer is nothing, there is more than one imperative to be found within it. Optimism and nihilism—and city and desert, and murder and suicide—are more of the entwined opposites supporting Didion's vision of existence. As movies and dreams are one, as pulp and literature, as development and destruction, so for Maria the idealism of the gambler is the deepest form of cynicism. Maria says that her father taught her to see life as a crap game. "It goes as it lays, don't do it the hard way," she would hear him say in her mind. It is clear that the real estate and motion picture deals that built Los Angeles—the giant casino of the entertainment industry that will trade on every murder and mentally ill child star—have truly made something out of nothing, of a desert city that will be desert again, from ash to ash returning.

Maria doesn't commit suicide, deciding instead to keep going, empowered by her intimacy with nothingness, treating life like the gamble that it is. She has found it necessary to excise the sentimentality from her life, those lies that form the connective tissue between events, that make our perception like a movie rather than a cutting-room experience: the story. "Fuck it, I said to them all, a radical surgeon of my own life," Maria says. "Never discuss. Cut." She is cutting the same narratives and received truths that Didion rejects in her motel room in Death Valley in "On Morality," when her mind resists abstraction and "veers inflexibly toward the particular." I had started collecting my own particulars as I sat by Echo Park Lake and read Didion, and weren't they, in their own way, cinematic? The old people I saw sitting on a piece of cardboard by the lake, hugging; the dragonfly fumbling to escape the nets covering the lily pads; the married couple on *Dateline* who named their house Happy Camp Ranch before the husband killed the wife. Maria insists that these kinds of shots and snatches of dialogue are "not a movie," but I disagree: What is film but the most disjointed art form there is, a collection of images edited together in jagged succession? Once I left my cell phone on my bedside table while I sat by the lake all day. I came home to several text messages from my mom saying that my dad had fallen off his bike and broken a rib. They were keeping him in the hospital overnight to monitor him. Was this the moment I, the auteur of my own life, had waited for, the one that explained my dread? When you are out of reach, that's when the danger catches up to your family. But in the tank-top weather beneath the leaning palm trees, as I watched the ducks and pedal boats and lotus blossoms, my character of myself wondered, and I did, too: Was this my fault, did I cause it to happen?

The Dream

In the spring of my first year in L.A., I would walk a mile and a half north from my apartment in Koreatown to Santa Monica Boulevard and the strange oasis of Hollywood Forever Cemetery. I would often talk to my mom on the phone when I went there, wandering so fretfully that I would get lost among the graves. Hollywood Forever is sixty acres in the middle of East Hollywood behind the Paramount lot. In fact, Paramount bought its land from the park in the early twentieth century, when it was still Hollywood Memorial Park Cemetery. It's a tourist destination, famous for housing stars like Rudolph Valentino and Iron Eyes Cody and two of the Ramones. Legendary director Cecil B. DeMille is buried with his wife, Constance, in a pair of giant Arthurian tombs. Tyrone Power's grave quotes from *Hamlet*, the "Good night, sweet prince" speech, of course.

But the fancy pedigree of its inhabitants is not immediately apparent on entering. It contains a historic Jewish burial ground, Beth Olam, and the rows of monuments with non-famous Jewish names and Stars of David were the first ones

I noticed. The cemetery is very close to Little Armenia, and there are large sections of granite markers with Armenian names and etchings of the dead in their Sunday best staring out unnervingly. Many of the monuments are truly old, from before the birth of the Los Angeles motion picture industry, when Los Angeles meant something completely different.

At times my eye would catch on a large or ornate monument (this is irritating because it is, by design, the rich exercising their control even after death) or a famous name, but the overall feeling there is unlike gawking down the Hollywood Walk of Fame. As in most cemeteries, chaos reigns in Hollywood Forever—the graves go in every direction, so crowded in some places that they resemble some sort of long-term storage, as if jumbled together there only until they are moved to their real plots. Peacocks swagger around the grounds, indifferent to visitors. Hollywood Forever is quirky and beautiful and more than the celebrity it is known for, just like Los Angeles.

Jules Roth, the crook owner of Hollywood Memorial from 1939 until his death in 1998, allowed it to fall into shameful disrepair, its crematorium forced to shut down in 1974 after the botched cremation of Mama Cass Elliot. In 1998 two young developers, Tyler and Brent Cassity, bought Hollywood Memorial and renamed and rebranded it, focusing on making a center for cultural programs like concerts and summer movies. There the audience scans itself for famous faces and during intermissions can seek out famous names in the confused rows of graves.

But is that what Hollywood Forever is *about*? From the beginning, I had trouble reconciling my daily experience of

Los Angeles—as a young and changing city; as green and mountainous; as incredibly ethnically diverse, with a culture and population that is predominantly Latino—with the sun-bleached, valley-girlish, suburban sprawl-ish, cultureless, entertainment-industry glamourous idea I had of it before I moved there. Is this cemetery about celebrity? Is it about Los Angeles Judaism, about the city's ethnic enclaves, about its turn-of-the-century oligarchy? Does this depend on which iteration of the cemetery you believe—the bankrupt, shambolic Hollywood Memorial or the hip and cultured Hollywood Forever? Do these distinctions even apply, or is each just a version of the same story, the same history that built Los Angeles and allows it to continue? As with everything in Los Angeles, I'm learning, objects in the mirror are always closer than they appear.

Forest Lawn Memorial Park in Glendale is spacious and sprawling, five times the size of Hollywood Forever, styled as an English country estate. I've been there only once, on a freak 100-degree day in April, having been unwholesomely initiated into the Los Angeles way of death after so many afternoons in Hollywood Forever. When I entered its wrought-iron gates—the largest in the world, the cemetery claims—I saw rolling hills of grass unfurling from the main drive. As I approached, I was startled by the rows of bronze plaques against the green. That is what Forest Lawn is designed to be: the kind of cemetery where one is surprised by graves.

I walked the grounds for a few hours, wandering through

the cemetery's oldest graves, many of them bulky and embellished, from before the park's look was streamlined: since the middle of the twentieth century, everyone, no matter who they are, gets a uniform bronze marker. I visited the park's walled gardens, also filled with graves, and its bizarre themed sections, including, chillingly, Babyland, where infants are buried. It is true that many of the twentieth century's greatest stars are buried at the park, but they aren't luring tourists like Hollywood Forever: Michael Jackson, Clark Gable, and Jean Harlow are all memorialized in elite sections of the cemetery's mausoleum that are not open to the public. I was so overwhelmed by Forest Lawn's scale and the day's heat that I staggered straight from the cemetery to an Atwater Village bar, makeup and sunscreen streaking down my face.

As Ben Ehrenreich writes in his masterly *Los Angeles* magazine investigation of the business of dying in L.A., "The End: What Really Happens When You Die?," "Los Angeles holds a special place in the history of death." This is largely because of the fascination (and awe and disgust) Forest Lawn has elicited in its visitors. From the time it was acquired in 1912 by Dr. Hubert L. Eaton—known as "the Builder"—it was designed to be "as unlike other cemeteries as sunshine is unlike darkness." Eschewing the chaotic development of most cemeteries, the concept for Forest Lawn sprang fully formed from Eaton's imagination: from the replicas of English churches and reproductions of Leonardo's sculptures to the cemetery's system of zoning, "a rigid real estate hierarchy," says Ehrenreich, "that reflects L.A.'s own." This is integral to the cemetery's business model, as it manufactures a demand for plots in certain areas of the park and so justifies their exorbitant price tags.

One of the park's most enthusiastic and horrified explorers was the English novelist Evelyn Waugh, who called it "a completely unique place—the only thing in California that is not a copy of something else." (Never mind all of the architectural and artistic imitation it contains.) Waugh came to Hollywood in 1947 to develop an adaptation of his novel *Brideshead Revisited* for MGM Studios. He found the movie industry and the United States generally to be completely distasteful, but he took perverse pleasure in learning about Glendale's giant cemetery ("morticians are the *only* people worth knowing," he wrote to a friend) and the American funeral industry. His short novel about Forest Lawn, *The Loved One*, is one of the most brutal and hilarious satires ever written about American culture. In it, Waugh invents unholy marvels of American engineering like Kaiser's Stoneless Peaches, which taste to the story's British poet hero, Dennis Barlowe, like "a ball of damp, sweet, cotton-wool." Waugh also writes endlessly of the convenience and indistinguishability of American women, so that they seem to manifest from the same American mania for mass production. Dennis wonders as he stares at a woman's leg, "Which came first in this strange civilization . . . the foot or the shoe, the leg or the nylon stocking?"

Forest Lawn, or as Waugh fictionalized it, Whispering Glades, is a pure and disturbing expression of this American sterility and consumerism. Waugh mimics the cemetery's relentlessly positive and euphemistic corporate language.

The Builder is figured in *The Loved One* as "the Dreamer." "Let me explain the Dream," is how the Mortuary Hostess begins her discussion of funeral arrangements with Dennis. Corpses are known as "Loved Ones," so a makeup artist says to an embalmer, "Here is the strangulated Loved One for the Orchid Room." Waugh was particularly appalled by the prevalence of embalming in the United States. As Ehrenreich points out, the draining of a corpse's bodily fluids and its preservation with formaldehyde "is practiced nowhere else in the world with the near universality that it achieved in North America." For Waugh, embalming nullified any memento mori, as "the body does not decay; it lives on, more chic in death than ever before, in its indestructible class A steel and concrete shelf." This was the true horror of Forest Lawn: its cheery but enfeebled idea of death, one designed to appeal to the American capitalist. "Dr. Eaton is the first man to offer eternal salvation at an inclusive charge as part of his under-taking service," wrote Waugh.

But America in *The Loved One* is not only consumerist and unnatural; it is also dispossessed. Waugh is conscious of the ethnic diversity of American names as remnants of iden-tities lost: there are characters named Otto Baumbein and Lorenzo Medici, Miss Mavrocordato and Mr. Van Gluck. Barlow's American paramour, a cosmetician at Whispering Glades, is named Aimee Thanatogenos, which, if my French and Greek serve me, can be roughly translated as "the Loved One," at least in the way Whispering Glades used the phrase. Aimee is Waugh's quintessential American orphan, named by unreliable parents after legendary Los Angeles televangelist Aimee Semple McPherson.

In Waugh's novel the United States is a land of transients, shorn of their previous identities and their history. Dennis is a World War II veteran, and he is "of a generation which enjoys a vicarious intimacy with death." He is presumably drawn to Whispering Glades, however unwillingly, because it displays that same brazen comfort with death. In Ehrenreich's essay, he describes how nineteenth-century Europeans rejected the earlier visibility of death in their culture, making it something "shameful and forbidden." One reason Europeans continue to be so dumbfounded by Los Angeles's enormous cemeteries is their spectacular resistance to the modern Western trend of making death and its reminders smaller, less grand, more separate from society. In Waugh's depiction, Forest Lawn effaces death in other ways: by stopping the effects of decay, by simplifying ideas of the afterlife. But it is still "a necropolis of the age of the Pharaohs," as Waugh wrote, "created in the middle of the impious twentieth century." Perhaps it reflects American identity not only in its capitalist model, but in a comfort with death that reflects the two violent and contradictory centuries of the United States's existence, where the dreams of the founders are still used to excuse every sin of conquest.

I was wandering Hollywood Forever again when I discovered the corner of the park dedicated to the Otis-Chandler family, the legendary owners of the *Los Angeles Times*. Harrison

Gray Otis, the first successful publisher of the paper, is buried beneath a mammoth obelisk. His son-in-law and heir, Harry Chandler, gets a curving marble slab flanked with urns and a pair of bald eagles. And among the rosebushes and religious statues shading the Otis-Chandler graves, I found a disconcerting monument, another marble structure topped with a bronze sculpture of an eagle perched on its aerie, preparing for flight. OUR MARTYRED MEN reads the adorning plaque, in memory of the men who "fell at their posts in The Times Building on the awful morning of October first, 1910—victims of conspiracy, dynamite and fire—The Crime of the Century."

The what?

I had never heard about the *Los Angeles Times* bombing of 1910, in which twenty-one of the paper's employees, "defenders of Industrial Freedom under Law," as the plaque puts it, were killed by a bomb planted by the Structural Iron Workers Union. Neither had anyone I informally surveyed after my discovery: my mother, brothers, or boyfriend. I was perplexed that my entire education, which includes, for what it's worth, a bachelor's degree in history, had neglected a terrorist attack on a major U.S. newspaper, an attack so traumatic that it had once been considered "the crime of the century." But it is starting to seem fitting to me that I found evidence of this trauma only in a graveyard. Monuments do not serve only to help us remember. They also allow us to forget and move on.

Howard Blum wrote about the attack in his 2008 book *American Lightning*, tracking three American icons as they converged at downtown Los Angeles's Alexandria Hotel at the time of the bombing: Billy Burns, the "American Sherlock Holmes," whose agency tracked down the bombers; Clarence Darrow, the great populist attorney, who defended the bombers; and D. W. Griffith, the father of American cinema. The most interesting parts of the book are the chronicles of Burns's and his operatives' remarkable (and for Burns, characteristically illegal) detective work. Burns connected bomb sites in Los Angeles and Illinois, tracked a suspect using a pile of sawdust, trailed anarchists for months in a colony on Puget Sound, used the first bugged microphone to listen in on jailhouse conversations, kidnapped and tortured witnesses, and extrajudicially extradited the bombers, J. J. McNamara and his brother J. B., to California.

Despite these compelling details, *American Lightning* draws shallow conclusions from the events it re-creates so vividly. The *Times* attack was the most dramatic in the Structural Iron Workers' massive bombing campaign, in which they dynamited over a hundred scab sites all over the United States. They sought to economically devastate Harrison Gray Otis, the paper's fervently anti-union publisher. Blum asserts that the McNamara trial ended the war between capital and labor and "helped move America into the modern world." "Entrepreneurial opportunities took shape," he writes breezily, "and they spread through the nation's cities and towns as a more hopeful alternative to the desperation of violence." Blum's optimistic, restorative reading of the situation is even more bizarre considering that the bombing occurred ninety years before the crime of *this* century, and the two attacks bear a ghostly similarity.

Blum's picture of twentieth-century America, which is built mostly on ideals rather than reality, finds a unique reflection in Los Angeles, the quintessential twentieth-century city. Much of *American Lightning* focuses on Otis, the publisher who helped to transform "a drab mud and adobe town of 11,000" in 1882 into a metropolitan center whose population was 900,000 at the time of the bombing. Otis was loathed by everyone who stood in the way of his dreams for Los Angeles, from the socialists whose unions he saw as obstructing industry to the farmers whose land he sought to develop as real estate. He figured himself as a military leader, calling himself "the General" and his house "the Bivouac," leading a campaign of mini–manifest destiny that included Los Angeles's annexing San Pedro and Wilmington in order to create its port.

Joan Didion, in "Times Mirror Square," her 1990 essay on the history of the *Los Angeles Times*, writes how Otis and his descendants exerted tremendous influence, using the *Times* as a platform not only to champion the growth of the city but also to increase their personal wealth. Didion describes how the development of downtown L.A. and the San Fernando Valley, the Southern California aerospace industry, Caltech, the 1932 Olympics, the Hollywood Bowl, and the freeway system all have their origins in "the impulse to improve Chandler property."

"The extent to which Los Angeles was literally invented by the *Los Angeles Times* and by its owners [. . .] remains hard for people in less recent parts of the country to fully apprehend," Didion writes. This is a city begotten from an idea, as Forest Lawn was begotten from the mind of the Builder, and it relies heavily on the idea to sustain it. This founding concept is a dream of limitless growth, an acquisitive spirit sowing tract houses and strip malls across the desert just as Forest Lawn paves the hills of Glendale with bronze plaques. The dream intertwined from the start with the city's most troubling aspects—its sprawl and its lack of natural resources—countering any difficulties these presented, so that image and reality are locked in eternal tension. This is why all true explorations of the Los Angeles condition express, as Didion writes, "how fragile the idea of the place was and how easily it could be lost."

The spring of my second year in California, my boyfriend and I went to a massive exhibition of movie costumes put on by the Academy of Motion Picture Arts and Sciences. On display were Indiana Jones's hat and whip, Holly Golightly's little black dress, Mary Poppins's umbrella, and the Dude's pajama pants. The exhibition's finale, after winding its way through costumes from *Fight Club*, *The Hunger Games*, *Cleopatra*, and *Star Wars*, was a little shrine set into the wall where visitors formed long lines to look at the ruby slippers Dorothy wore in *The Wizard of Oz*. I leaned into the glass in awe of the red sequin character shoes, so tiny and so fragile.

It occurs to me how much we resembled medieval pilgrims, traveling to see relics of our beloved teenage martyr, Saint Judy of the Yellow Brick Road. It is morbid to want to see things that famous people touched and wore, Charlie Chaplin's bowler and pleated pants containing the idea of his body the same way a sarcophagus would. This hoarding of artifacts seems like a natural activity for the guardians of the motion picture industry, who are in the business of collecting ghosts. The very technology of film carries a kind of resurrection, capturing the past with a scary depth and intimacy, fourteen-year-old Judy Garland still as adorable and vulnerable today as she was in 1939. If we look at it this way, Los Angeles takes on a necrophiliac quality: it is home to several of the largest cemeteries in the world and to the industry that both manufactures American celebrity and sweeps up its traces.

In *American Lightning*, Blum writes that D. W. Griffith's groundbreaking 1915 film *The Birth of a Nation* "would help America—its art, its ideals, its imagination—move into the modern world." He doesn't attempt to reconcile this with his understanding of the film as regressive and disturbing, "an odd, sour, and disturbingly racist reinterpretation of the Civil War and Reconstruction." *American Lightning* takes its name from Woodrow Wilson's apocryphal review of *Birth of a Nation*, that it was like "writing history with lightning," which does a lot to embody the film's contradictions. Lightning is scary, beautiful, powerful, ephemeral, unreliable, dangerous, and mysterious: not a good thing, in other words, to write history with at all. A landmark of cultural innovation depicting a hateful revisionist history pushes irony to the point of combustion. Griffith was the person who brought the movies to Los Angeles, and the fraught spirit of the first Hollywood blockbuster still inhabits competing versions of L.A.: it is either a future city, constantly paving over its past, or an enormous archive or crypt, a dusty repository of American icons.

Early in *American Lightning*, Billy Burns describes a juicy theory of the *Los Angeles Times* bombing. It deals with the scheme to divert water from the Owens River Valley on the Nevada border 250 miles to Los Angeles. Los Angeles voters, after much passionate goading from the *Times*, had approved $22.5 million in bonds to fund the creation of the aqueduct, but at the time of the bombings, Harrison Gray Otis was about to double down on a water scheme that would make him and his business partners millions.

Otis, using the front of the Los Angeles Suburban Homes Company, had been buying and developing cheap land in the desert stretches of the San Fernando Valley, north of L.A. They would use water from the Owens aqueduct to make the valley habitable. But their plan had encountered obstacles: the aqueduct was still not finished, and citizens would have to approve more bonds for its completion. The Socialist Party was gaining traction with Los Angeles voters, and they disapproved of "handing the aqueduct water over to the land barons." If Socialists prevailed in the 1911 mayoral election, Otis and the Suburban Homes Company would have no water for the houses they had spent so much to build in the valley. As Blum explains, Burns proposed that Otis himself was behind the bombing of the *Times* building. Otis had recently taken out a large insurance policy on it, money that would help buoy him while the aqueduct was completed. And by blaming labor for the bombing, he would tarnish the reputation of their Socialist allies, ruining their chances in the 1911 elections.

This was completely wrong, as it turns out. The McNamaras, radical labor activists, were behind the attacks, and they did hurt the Socialists' place in Los Angeles politics, handing Otis his goal of a developed San Fernando Valley, a testament to his good luck. Still, it makes an irresistible story, a solution Blum probably would have chosen for his mystery if he hadn't been constrained by fact. It has the hallmarks of a classic noir tale, all of which take place in cities where corruption is the rule, not an aberration. The only thing the story lacks is the noir impulse to, as Faye Dunaway memorably says in 1974's *Chinatown*, "*cherchez la femme.*"

My roommate my first spring in Los Angeles was an actor and a carpenter who would leave for weeks at a time to film bit parts in B movies. I lodged myself in front of his giant TV during his time away, watching *Chinatown* in between seasons of *The Mindy Project*, treating the movie like the piece of broccoli a steakhouse gives you with your porterhouse: a grudging concession to good taste, if not tastiness.

Chinatown, though, played perfectly into the story of early Los Angeles that I was piecing together through its cemeteries. The film is a noir-ification of the plot to bring Owens River water to Los Angeles. In it, the chief engineer at the Los Angeles Department of Water and Power, Hollis Mulwray, is murdered after he publicly opposes plans to build a reservoir. Private detective Jake Gittes (Jack Nicholson channeling Philip Marlowe), working with Mulwray's widow, Evelyn, uncovers a complicated plot by Mulwray's

former partner and Evelyn's father, Noah Cross. They plan
to buy up land in the San Fernando Valley using the names
of senile retirees and to covertly and illegally irrigate it using
Los Angeles's water. In the film's ending, it trades a noir aesthetic for a Gothic one: Cross is a true villain who has raped
Evelyn and fathered her daughter. Evelyn, as it turns out, is
not a femme fatale. The film's surprise is in how tightly the
apparent system of power holds fast, how straightforward
allegiances are and how little our heroes can do in the face
of corrupt authority. Melodramatic as it is, *Chinatown* is a
weirdly apt depiction of a city that was developed by a hand-
ful of powerful men who did not have much use for rules or
ethics.

In *American Lightning*, Blum writes about the early tri-
umph of Griffith's short film *A Corner in Wheat*. It featured
an ambitious parallel structure, following "farmers stoically
working in a field; the Wheat King hatching his plot to control the market; and the city's downtrodden poor hoping to
buy bread," sending a poignant message about the power im-
balance in the relationship between America's landowners,
producers, and consumers. The film is based on *The Pit*, the
second novel in what Frank Norris planned as an epic trilogy
(he died before completing the third) that began with 1901's
The Octopus, a true California story that, in California
fashion, is more complicated than the patterns *A Corner in
Wheat* would distill from it.

In her 2004 meditation on California identity, *Where I
Was From*, Didion spends significant time trying to make
sense of *The Octopus*. On its surface, it is an anti-corporate

novel about the megalithic power of the railroad to control
and abuse the humble farmer. A pivotal scene involves a
shootout between ranchers in the San Joaquin Valley and
federal marshals hired by the Southern Pacific railroad to
evict them. But these conflicts are not as allegorical as they
may appear. Crucially, these ranchers were, as Didion writes,
"in no sense simple farmers." They were entrepreneurs who
had come to California seeking a fortune from its fecundity
in the same way Gold Rush spectators had tried to exploit
its mineral resources, and their business plans were depen-
dent on their proximity to railroad routes. "The only actual
conflict in *The Octopus*," Didion writes, "turns out to be
between successful and failed members of the same entrepreneurial class." This recalls incestuous themes in *Chinatown*,
as parties that seem to be opponents were in fact closely
aligned. The development of Southern California followed
no traditional narratives: it was uniquely intentional, flowing
from a singular energy, serving the interests of a certain
small population of men, whether Harrison Gray Otis, Noah
Cross, or the Railroad King. It occurs to me that these subverted narratives are what kept me wandering Los Angeles's
cemeteries, which, in their differences, all serve to memori-
alize these men and their philosophies, ironically bespeaking
a belief in real estate, in staking your claim, in insisting on
permanence if you can't have eternity.

And the infighting among these men is another distrac-
tion from what has always been the real California conflict.
As Didion succinctly explains,

the octopus, if there is one, turns out to be neither
the railroad nor corporate ownership but indifferent nature.

This was what Burns knew when devising his theory that
the *L.A. Times* bombing was an inside job. In Los Angeles, the
imperative is not to *cherchez la femme*; it is to *cherchez*
the water.

The Octopus **begins** on a day when "all the vast reaches of
the San Joaquin Valley—in fact all South Central California,
was bone dry, parched, and baked and crisped after four
months of cloudless weather." More than a century later,
this description bears down on the San Joaquin like a death
sentence. In the spring of 2014, a *Los Angeles Times* feature described how extreme drought conditions devastated
families of migrant farmworkers. Waves of farmers fled to
California from Oklahoma, Texas, Missouri, and Arkansas
during the disastrous droughts of the 1930s; now farmworkers are migrating away from Southern California's
own dust bowl. Communities in the San Joaquin are fading,
in danger of becoming ghost towns.

In summer 2014, drought covered 100 percent of California, with 76 percent of the state experiencing extreme drought
conditions. These are remarkable and terrifying circumstances, prime for forest fires and agricultural devastation.
But it is hard to look at a drought as an emergency—it quickly
becomes the new normal. A farmworker in the *Los Angeles*

Times article said, "Drought is different from other natural disasters because it doesn't end." My boyfriend laughed when we saw a sign on the 101 reading SERIOUS DROUGHT. DON'T WASTE WATER. "I thought it said 'serious thought,'" he said. Well, I reminded him, it *is* a serious thought.

It took me two buses and almost two hours to get to Boyle Heights, the East Los Angeles neighborhood where Evergreen Memorial Park and Crematory is nestled. Established in 1877, it is the oldest graveyard in Los Angeles and one of the largest, housing 300,000 graves in its sixty-seven acres. Its Garden of the Pines is a monument to Japanese pioneers, and rows of beautiful Japanese graves lace through the rest of the park like veins. It is different from other Los Angeles cemeteries. It feels less preened, more chaotic. Its grass grows sometimes green, sometimes yellow, straggling in dehydrated patches or failing altogether, revealing expanses of bare dirt. Amid the Japanese graves are monuments to L.A.'s early patriarchs, or as Ehrenreich puts it in "The End," a "stratum of dead whites with streets named after them." This includes John Edward Hollenbeck, who sold the city the land that would become Exposition Park, and Theodore Rimpau, whose massive Rancho Las Cienegas became much of West Los Angeles. Isaac Lankershim and Isaac Newton Van Nuys are also buried there, Otis Chandler's collaborators in the Los Angeles Suburban Homes Company and the scheme to develop the San Fernando Valley. There are layers of irony here: the graves of men who went to great lengths to keep Los Angeles evergreen grow up amid yellow grass in a cemetery called Evergreen. When I was there, I saw a family gathered around a grave, somehow watering it with a hose.

Evergreen illustrates why its men with streets named after them had to dream up Los Angeles so completely, lending the city the same artificiality that Waugh disdained in Forest Lawn. Los Angeles is not a city that could ever have existed naturally—that is, given its natural resources—in its current form. In "Half in Love with Easeful Death," Waugh makes a confident prediction about the end of Los Angeles. "It will be destroyed by drought," he writes. "Bones will whiten along the Santa Fe Trail as the great recession struggles Eastwards. Nature will re-assert herself and the seasons gently obliterate the vast, deserted suburb." It was obvious to him that Los Angeles's hyperdevelopment was no match for indifferent nature.

Los Angeles's enormous cemeteries are emblems of the city's excessive nature, its belief in relationships of space and growth that exist only in the physics of dreams. But they also embody Los Angeles's relationship with destruction. Engineered to be a tropical paradise, a verdant ocean city enjoying everlasting youth, its citizens carry on in spite of the imminence of many natural emergencies, including droughts, fires, mudslides, and earthquakes. Its giant cemeteries are both an attempt to control death and evidence of the city's strange comfort with it. As Didion writes in her essay "Los Angeles Days," "Something in the human spirit rejects planning on a daily basis for catastrophe."

Moving to Los Angeles from a small town in Montana, I

marvel at how quickly I got used to budgeting driving time, adding hours to my day where I was doing essentially nothing; to two-hour cross-city bus rides; to the smog and the white sun and their attending migraines. I realized from other people's Internet posts that I didn't feel an earthquake because I was on an already shaking bus riding down Third Street in Mid-City; instead of fear, I felt light disappointment, and kept scrolling on Twitter. California's drought scared me because I had already gotten used to it, as I had the rest of my new city's inconveniences. It wasn't invisible to me, and adjusting to small miseries did not mean I was not miserable.

I do not think of Los Angeles with my fellow transplant Waugh's same disgust. I love it in its striving and its failing. But like Waugh, I looked to the city's cemeteries for what is both its signature and its fatal flaw: a dream so ironclad it endeavors to reject even the Big Buzzkill. On the plaque in Hollywood Forever, the *Los Angeles Times* finally wishes farewell to its "martyred men": "Forever green be the turf which California, through all her perennial summertimes, will graciously spread above their cherished graves!" It's the poetry of denial: the people of Los Angeles know their weather is not an eternal summer, but the heat of a desert waiting to reclaim it. The grass is not forever. Neither are the graves.

Part 3

Weird Sisters

A Teen Witch's Guide
to Staying Alive

My first formal dalliance with witchcraft was in fourth grade, though my suspicions that I was magic came much earlier. As a small child, I would tighten my concentration on objects, thinking I might move them with my mind. I engaged in experiments in mind reading, which, if you don't let your subject in on it, is easy to tell yourself you are doing successfully. At the same time I also engaged in schoolyard charlatanism, shoving the planchette around when we played with the Ouija board and convincing a gullible friend that I communicated with leprechauns, a ruse that went off so well I had to continue it for years. The imagination as the source of childhood "magic" is the cliché that drives basically all youth entertainment. In that case, *magic* means nothing more than *control*.

My best friend in fourth grade was a new girl in school who was pale as paper, with butt-length red hair. Her dad was a giant in a leather jacket who listened to Led Zeppelin, like my big brother; her stepmom had a strange fantasy-novel name derived from Greek mythology. They were Wiccans, she told me, but warned me to tell no one at our small Idaho school. "I'm a witch in training," she wrote in tiny handwriting in my diary.

> *I can't cast spells yet. I'm not a full witch.* No one can know what I tell Alice. *When I'm completely trained I get the following: a magic sword, altar, a lead mini of Diana, the moon goddess, and everything that goes on an altar.*

The idea of witchcraft as a religious practice was news to me, and it seemed like a fantastic work-around to the necessity of inborn supernatural gifts. The drama of secrecy and potential ostracization made Wicca all the more appealing.

My friend lent me the 1990s occult classic *Teen Witch* by Silver RavenWolf, which I hid self-importantly under my bed. The book taught me to jerry-rig a Wiccan altar from household items. I found a yellow clipboard and placed on it a statue of the Virgin Mary (to represent the goddess) and a candle shaped like a recycling bin that I found in the bargain section at Claire's. In my first act as witch in training, I cast a circle of power, a sovereign region of happiness in my bedroom. I walked in a circle, focusing so intensely on the magic flowing from my index finger to the floor that I could almost see it.

I bought a used copy of *Teen Witch* on Amazon recently, careful to get one that preserved its iconic first-edition cover.

It's a painting of five witchy teens in the greatest hits of nineties fashion: backward baseball caps, velour, thigh-highs, mom jeans, crop tops, overalls, a yin-yang chain belt. It has served as a great coffee table book, but I reread it with much more seriousness than I approached it with when I was nine. Just as RavenWolf begs her readers, I did not jump around or skip straight to the spells she includes, but solemnly read her baby's guide to witchcraft cover to cover.

RavenWolf brags that she is "one of the most famous witches in the United States today," and she has written more than a dozen magic how-to books. Reading her homely, mom-ish prose, I feel sure that RavenWolf had little to do with the marketing of this book. The edgy styling of the kids on its cover seems to contradict her efforts to dissuade nineties teens from thinking witchcraft is another Goth fashion accessory. She explains that Wicca is a source of positivity, that the only legitimate magic helps others and connects a person to the greater Spirit. It is, in other words, just another religion, and one that RavenWolf suggests is best practiced quietly.

Many of the spells she includes are nothing more than faintly cloaked practical advice. In her "Glamour Spell," she tells her readers, "If someone is making fun of you because you smell, maybe you do. Keep your gym clothes clean. Use a spray in your sneakers." Many of her spells would be embarrassing to be caught performing. A spell to treat cuts and scrapes involves holding a hand over the hurt area and repeating, "Owie-fix, owie-fix / You're the fairy that I pick. Bring the healing / Come right quick!" Her "Turn Back Poverty Spell" is just writing "I banish poverty" on seven pieces of toilet paper and flushing them down the toilet.

A lot of RavenWolf's folk magic instructions feel like the compulsions anxious children take part in anyway: obsessive praying, carrying lucky objects, hiding things. Her "My Castle Spells" are several ideas for magical protections for the Teen Witch's house, including chanting and making the sign of the pentacle over every window and door in the house every night. This legitimizes the restless avenues anxiety takes, the rituals of vigilance and control children are prone to.

I'm reminded of Merricat, the teenage witch who narrates Shirley Jackson's *We Have Always Lived in the Castle*, as she describes her own protective magic: "Always on Wednesday mornings I went around the fence. It was necessary for me to check constantly to be sure that the wires were not broken and the gates were securely locked." I read *We Have Always Lived in the Castle* twice the same fall I revisited *Teen Witch*, in my house in the San Bernardino National Forest, high in the gloomy mountains above Southern California's Inland Empire, having exchanged smog for fog. I was working as the poet in residence at a boarding school there, and I leaned into the enigmatic eccentricity I felt was expected of my new role. I engaged in all kinds of casual divination, having my students wander the woods looking for sticks shaped like letters and attempt to communicate with Gertrude Stein's ghost on a homemade Ouija board. And I was alone in my cabin in the woods and scared of ghosts, animals, and murderers: I was unable to read Jackson's ghost story *The Haunting of Hill House* at night in my bed because, I realized with a shiver,

I was also living in an isolated *house* on a *hill*. In short, I returned to the magic and magical thinking of my youth, for reasons both whimsical and less so. In Jackson's strange New England fairy tale, Merricat's is a neurotic magic, as she catalogs the objects she's buried in the acres of wilderness that her family owns: "my marbles and my teeth and my colored stones, all perhaps turned to jewels by now, held together under the ground in a powerful taut web which never loosened, but held fast to guard us."

She wants to protect herself and what's left of her family— her older sister, Constance, and her feeble uncle, Julian—from the ignorant townspeople in the hostile village beyond their land. Merricat is one in a long line of literary tomboys, taking her place beside Scout Finch, Harriet the Spy, and Jo March. But Jackson twists this archetype, imbuing her tomboy with a sinister mixture of alchemy and fear. When Merricat's routine is threatened early in the book, she immediately reacts by smashing a milk pitcher, as smashing things into glittering shards is one source of her power. Her feral girl magic is far from RavenWolf's benign Teen Witches. We learn that someone poisoned her father, mother, younger brother, and aunt years earlier, and Merricat is the reader's only suspect. This is Jackson's uneasy feat in the book: readers' sympathetic intimacy with our strange and murderous teenage narrator.

One thing that endears Merricat to us is her loyalty to her angelic older sister, Constance, an avatar of purity and nurturing domesticity. Constance does nothing but cook, clean, and garden, and she is perfectly attuned to the cycles of nature and the harvest. Jackson is leading us to wonder whether Constance is partaking in her own kind of magic. Observing Constance's rows and rows of preserved fruits and vegetables in their cellar, Merricat tells her, "You bury food the way I bury treasure." Both witchcraft and food preservation are traditionally feminine arts and safeguards, ways of staying alive. After cleaning their house, Merricat describes herself and Constance as "carrying our dustcloths and the broom and dustpan and mop like a pair of witches walking home." It is easy to forget that the accouterments of witchcraft—the broomstick, the cauldron—are traditionally found around the hearth, the woman's domain.

Merricat and Constance enact their food fetish at the dinner table and in the garden and in their magic. Jackson and so many other writers rely on food and feeding as a particularly overt, if poignant, metaphor. In *Beloved*, Toni Morrison also writes about two agoraphobic women haunted by a murder in their family, shut out by their community, bound together by guilt and need. When Morrison's protagonist, Sethe, who has run away from slavery, is reunited with her children, she has "milk enough for all" in her still-lactating breasts, embodying the first imperative of motherhood. Throughout *Beloved*, eating metaphors are both loud and quiet. Sethe is consumed with grief, actually saying, "I'm going to eat myself." When the ghost of her dead daughter comes back, the girl is ravenous for everything she can get from Sethe: her food, her attention, her men, her body. But when it comes to women's relationships to eating, the significance is not just metaphorical. Merricat dislikes eating in front of other people at all. In this refusal, she resembles many teenage girls. I guess we are talking about magic again (or do I mean compulsion?) when we talk about food as a domain of feminine control.

In Elissa Washuta's 2015 book *Starvation Mode*, which she calls "A Memoir of Food, Consumption, and Control," she describes how her lifelong food obsession was connected to her untamable emotions. "Only cry if you are hurt or scared," a rule remembered from her childhood, caused nothing but confusion. "While I knew how to count to three," she writes, "I did not know the boundaries of pain and fear." Her food compulsions—from tasting a salt lick she found in the forest as a child to the bingeing, restriction, and obsessive dieting she vacillated between for years—all had the same appeal: "to beckon toward the impossible dream of making my own microscopic and mysterious cells change according to my will."

Washuta's book is revelatory on women's disordered relationships with food, a subject that would seem to have been covered. She describes how her first "diet," a dangerous 600-calorie-a-day restriction, made her feel empowered and safe, "like good St. Catherine in her iron girdle." Eating disorders are a kind of penance and a kind of fortification and a kind of disguise. It is a paradox of womanhood that women have been so long associated with the private sphere, the home and the family, while our bodies are considered public property. In the climax of *We Have Always Lived in the Castle*, Merricat sets fire to her house to oust her hateful cousin, Charles, from her space, ironically opening the house to the citizens of the village, who invade it first to put out the fire and second to ransack it, smashing and destroying all of the sisters' belongings. "It seemed that all the wealth and hidden treasure of our house had been found out and torn and soiled," Merricat says. What was private is made public.

In its most disordered form, Washuta's dieting in *Starvation Mode* is transformed from an enforcement of the male gaze to a kind of purifying fire, reducing her body to what cannot be consumed or destroyed. "I wanted a body that was a plywood box," she writes, "one that, even if it were broken open, might be full of nothing fragile." In the same way, the fire has diminished Merricat and Constance's house to its necessary parts, the areas that revolve around food: the kitchen, the cellar, and the garden. Like in the hunger-addled body, they have achieved a unity of fortification and vulnerability, a perfect isolation, as their house becomes "a castle, turreted and open to the sky." Washuta's and Jackson's are both disturbing solutions to an embattled female existence. It is upsetting, to say the least, to confront Jackson's vision of the essence of human life as eking comfort from constant hostility, attrition, and ruin. Jackson's work consistently explores the dark mysteries of scale one can discover in the descent into agoraphobia: that a house can be a world, and a body can be a house.

As I read *Starvation Mode* in my cabin's fluorescent-lit kitchen, on flimsy Walmart furniture the boarding school provided for me, eating six dried apricots cut in quarters and mixed with a half cup of plain yogurt, the food obsession in the witch books I had been reading dawned on me uncomfortably. I had also been reading Helen Oyeyemi's Shirley Jackson homage *White Is for Witching*, which follows a teenage girl named Miranda whose eating disorder will allow her to eat chalk and little else. In this way she seems to eat the famous White Cliffs of her hometown of Dover, making her an earth witch if there ever was one. Miranda is unsure whether she embodies a witch in a fairy tale, monstrously hungry, feeding on souls and children. She seems more like Alice in Wonderland, eating but only growing smaller. Although *White Is for Witching* would appear to be a compassionate lens on a kind of girlish madness, here, too, an eating disorder spins out wildly into metaphor. The novel is an exploration of British imperialism's hunger for resources and for people, as Miranda and her foremothers, all of whom shared her compulsion to eat dirt, sticks, and rocks, are literally hungry for land. The book is not subtle: one of Miranda's grandmothers is shown wearing white, dressed as the personified Britannia. And Oyeyemi riffs on the ironic layers of meaning loaded in the color white, showing it as a color that consumes, that contains and assimilates all other colors: "White is for witching, a colour to be worn so that all other colours can enter you, so that you may use them." This is an elegant description of the white hand of the British Empire as it moved greedily across the globe.

This is another story of a girl trapped in a house, but Miranda is not agoraphobic. Her parents open a bed-and-breakfast in the house that has been in her mother's family for generations, and it is haunted by her female ancestors, all of whom are either cursed by or conspiring with the evil spirit of the house itself. The house is the narrator of much of the book, recounting how it tortures and controls Miranda and seeks in its racist mission to eject all nonwhite people from itself. It's like a hyperactive explosion of the Gothic, where the house is the ultimate symbol. The Gothic as a literary aesthetic is completely entwined with the sins of colonialism and the unwelcome and uncanny ways they manifested themselves in Europe. The chaotic forces in the Brontës' haunted-house stories are albatrosses of the colonial world, like the Caribbean madwoman Bertha Rochester and the dark changeling Heathcliff, whom other characters surmise could be Indian or American. In *White Is for Witching*, after the Kosovar immigrants who work for her father are driven out by her house's tormenting, Miranda realizes that they "lived in a different house from her when she thought they were all living in the same house." The house transparently stands in for British society, where the experience of those who have it hard is invisible to those who have it easy.

White Is for Witching is just as fanciful and indulgent and insane as it sounds. It proliferates indecisively with references to myths and fairy tales, not sure if Miranda is a wicked witch from Western fairy tales or the soucouyant, the evil hag in Caribbean folktales who eats children's souls. She is either Alice in Wonderland, Eurydice, or Narnia's White Witch. Or she might be an inversion of one of these familiar stories, a princess trying desperately to escape her fairy godmother. All of these narratives lay claim to Miranda's body, saddling her with the impossible weight of her people's ugly history. It's a cautionary tale for white women about what fairy-tale princesses actually inherit, another variation on "you break it, you bought it."

I didn't intend for this to become a term paper about how modern campfire stories about ghosts and witches have their roots in colonial guilt. The political—and yes, feminist—implications of fairy tales and ghost stories have, I think, been adequately established. But it still stands that some of our greatest writers, especially those who are interested in the problem of womanhood, have invented some of the weirdest witches and the angriest ghosts. *Beloved* is a book I would futilely argue about with kids at the boarding school, a work of unbelievable darkness, beauty, and complexity that languishes too often on high school syllabi. If my students were assigned a book in English class, they assumed they were supposed to slog through it and complain about it. I couldn't believe the thematic parallels between *Beloved* and *We Have Always Lived in the Castle*, especially since Jackson's book is often treated as some kind of quirky Goth YA, with ersatz Edward Gorey cover illustration, and *Beloved*, obviously, is not. But both books—through marketing and curriculum—are constantly wasted on teenagers.

In *Beloved*, Sethe escapes from slavery with her children, but she brutally murders her older daughter when she is caught in the North, both to spare her child the fate of slavery and to escape having to return herself. For years after that, her house is racked by her child's ghost, "full of baby's venom," a torment that stops only with the appearance of a mysterious young woman. Sethe takes her as the second coming of her dead daughter, whose tombstone read only BELOVED. Morrison's Beloved is a tragic and potent Dead

Girl as she dogs the mother who murdered her for a decade and eventually comes back to claim her.

It is a fair question whether Sethe is supernaturally haunted or psychologically haunted by the traumas she witnessed in slavery and the crime she committed to save her children from that same pain. She seems to be living within a sleepy shadow world thick with memories, symbols, magic, grief, and desire, especially in the house that she does not let her eighteen-year-old daughter, Denver, leave. Denver is the only person who has stayed with Sethe, cleft to her by necessity and fear: her grandmother is eight years dead when the book opens, and both of her brothers have run off. The symbolic significance of the house in *Beloved* is foremost as a womb for Denver's perverse prolonged gestation. When Paul D, whom Sethe knew in slavery, sees Denver, he says, "Last time I saw your mama, you were pushing out the front of her dress," and Sethe says that she still is. When I read the novel, I am drawn to Denver more than any other character, in the same way that we sympathize with the faithful son in the parable of the prodigal son in the Gospels. There are theories about the true identity of the young woman they take to be Beloved, whether she is a demon or a runaway from a nearby town. But to me she is always Denver's ghost.

When the house is in the ghost's thrall, quaking angrily, the furniture walking around of its own free will, it is the sublimated expression of Denver's rage at her mother. When the grown-up Beloved comes and devours Sethe's life, she is the full embodiment of Denver's love and hatred and want. The narration says that "years of haunting had dulled

[Denver];" this is meant to indicate Denver's *being* haunted, but it leaves the semantic possibility that she is also doing the haunting. There are indications that Beloved and Denver are shades of the same person, like when Beloved is staring at her reflection in a pond, and Denver's face joins hers in the water. "You think she was sure 'nough your sister?" Paul D asks Denver after Beloved is gone. "At times I think she was . . . more," she says. It is only once the dark emotions that have helped hold Denver hostage are released, once Beloved and Sethe are "locked in a love that wore everybody out," that Denver can make her escape into the outside world. Stories like *Beloved* and *We Have Always Lived in the Castle* are about how the rhythms of households can hold people like gravity. Denver must find a way to break her orbit around her mother, her binary star.

In *Beloved*, Morrison writes about how, after the Civil War, freed black women created makeshift households, "configurations and blends of families of women and children, while elsewhere, solitary, hunted and hunting for, were men, men, men." Women's lack of mobility is our weakness and our strength: we even now find it difficult to escape abuse and dysfunction, but we create networks of protection, rooted and secret. Morrison's novel is a testament to how black women authored the survival of black society after slavery, founding a matriarchy on all the violence and terror they'd been subjected to.

Sethe relies on the kindness of other women, like the poor white woman who massages her feet and helps to deliver Denver in the middle of the forest. Her neighbors cast her out after she murders her daughter, essentially isolating her and Denver in their house, but in her final showdown with Beloved, the community of black women are the ones who come to Sethe's aid, assembling to chase Beloved off. The women sing, "building voice upon voice . . . a wave of sound wide enough to sound deep water and knock the pods off chestnut trees. It broke over Sethe and she trembled like the baptized in its wash." These women love and protect their pariahs, recognizing them as essential elements in life's daily rhythm.

In Morrison's other most famous novel, *Sula*, when the title character returns to her village, she is instantly met with suspicion for having left, for being unmarried, independent, and educated. But her unwholesome presence, witchily announced with a plague of robins, immediately has a moralizing effect on the community. As they take part in rituals of "counter-conjure" against Sula's powerful magic, they also begin to "cherish their husbands and wives, protect their children, repair their homes." Morrison identifies this productive scapegoating as a kind of equanimity in the face of both happiness and tragedy from a people who had weathered one calamity after another, for whom "plague and drought were as 'natural' as springtime."

This spiritual equilibrium, a way of thinking much older than Christian ideas of darkness and light, produces all the twinning in these witch stories, women finding their equal and opposite halves: Denver and Sethe, Constance and Merricat. In *White Is for Witching*, Miranda starts dating a girl she meets at college named Ore who is ethnically Nigerian but was adopted by white parents. Although she is infatuated with Ore (literalizing the feeding theme in the book, she says she wants to eat her), Miranda's curse usurps their relationship. Ore seems to develop an eating disorder, too, and grows thinner and thinner, and when they go home to visit, Miranda's house is affronted by Ore's presence and tries to drive her out. One can read the book as a fairy tale about a girl, Ore, trying to escape the grips of a hungry witch, Miranda. In *Sula*, the best friends Sula and Nel share in their magic, too. As girls, they perform an intricate spell in which they dig holes in the ground with twigs and then bury bottle caps, cigarette butts, and other trash, and then, just after, they accidentally kill a tiny neighbor boy by flinging him into the rushing river. It's an indication that they are possessed of something powerful and dangerous, that they might be violating some social order with a "friendship [that] was so close, they themselves had difficulty distinguishing one's thoughts from the other's."

In adulthood, Nel is lured by the call of romantic love, finding in marriage not an uncanny closeness but the gift of someone who "saw her singly." Sula's magic grows big on its own, effecting strange calamities and luring men away from their wives with her powerful beauty, a birthmark looming over her eye looking either like a rose or a copperhead snake. Sula sleeps with Nel's husband out of a perverse desire to be close to her, mistakenly thinking that they still shared everything. Their friendship is over after that: Sula dies young, and

Nel grows old, haunted by her grief over her lost friend. It is difficult not to feel for Nel, who rejects her friend and her truest self in the process, collaborating with the rest of society to cast Sula out. If we expect women to enforce societal rules, their ruthlessness is a kind of survival, too.

I'll reiterate: it is upsetting, all of these imperfect or failed strategies for living while female. Sethe eventually finds redemption and freedom in romantic love, but Miranda dies, and Sula does, too. It's clear that if both good and bad witches are going to find ways to survive, their methods will not always be ones we approve of. Toward the end of her life, Shirley Jackson became so agoraphobic that she could not even leave her bedroom, and she wrote, shortly before her death, a novel that glorifies the agoraphobic instinct, about two sisters who are rightfully terrified of the outside world. In perhaps the most subversive element of *We Have Always Lived in the Castle*, Constance and Merricat live happily ever after. Merricat is afraid of the relentlessness of time and the inevitability of growing up, but she thrives in the daily and weekly circles of domestic time: routines of meals, chores, seasons. At the end of the book, she and Constance live and eat happily, harmonizing with their garden's growing cycles and consuming the talismanic preserves Constance buried in the earth. They are village legends: the townspeople tell one another scary stories about Constance and Merricat eating children, and they bring offerings of food to quell the sisters' anger, performing counter-conjure like the neighbors in *Sula*. The sisters become more witchy than ever before, hidden and alone in their spooky house on the edge of town.

As Washuta writes, she learned from the Disney movie *The Little Mermaid* "that romance hinged upon the girl's physical transformation to fit the prince's notion of perfection." When she was a little older, she learned how to enact that kind of transformation in teen magazines, which "seemed to follow an editorial assumption that every reader dieted, even if the practice was a passive state set in place by default." Those same teen magazines are where I first read about RavenWolf and her spells for teen witches, as if their only purpose was to provide more or less desperate remedies for teen-girl neuroses. In seventh grade we had to write down our worst fear, and I wrote "school shootings" and then quickly erased it, afraid someone would see and, deeper down, that writing it would make it come true: even seeing the words was scary. At that time, and before, I would write my anger and my self-hatred in my diary and then I would go back in later and destroy or deface the pages, sometimes writing mocking marginalia like I was my own bully. I was afraid to make my darkness real by writing it; reading my own dark thoughts was both embarrassing and rife with talismanic power. Revising my diary was a ritual to carve those feelings from myself, protecting my inner life even in a space that was supposed to be secret.

One of RavenWolf's protection spells is the "Chameleon Spell," to make the teen witch disappear. It is a meditation exercise, in which the spell caster must memorize a magic poem, "then practice making the edges of [herself] fuzzy while chanting the poem." This spell is, in other words, the same thing that girls do in hallways, classrooms, and walking down the street: close their eyes and pray to be less conspicuous, less exposed. This is why *We Have Always Lived in the Castle*'s fairy-tale ending is so moving. Jackson's weird sisters achieve what every teen witch seeks: if not love, at least invisibility.

And So It Is

The reality soap opera is a form that has been unfairly ignored by our popular critics. Even the masterpieces of the genre have not received their due, no in-depth analyses of the narrative techniques of *Jersey Shore* or *Laguna Beach* or *The Hills*. After the age of eight, when my parents made the questionable decision to allow me to have a TV in my room, I spent hours every day watching anything the pioneering producers at MTV found fit to put on the air. I was obsessed particularly with the classic *The Real World*, the first modern reality show, where attractive twentysomethings with widely varying lifestyles were forced to live together and got in constant, inevitable fights.

My uncle bought me a book about *The Real World* from Barnes & Noble and I studied it purposefully, preparing myself for when I turned eighteen and I could audition to be on it, which had quickly become my greatest dream. The book helpfully included the actual questionnaire that potential cast members had to fill out, including questions like "How important is sex to you?" and "What are your thoughts on affirmative action?" which I, as an elementary schooler, answered to the best of my ability. But beyond its most famous reality programming, MTV has made more addictive and sublime reality shows than I can list, including *Rich Girls*, in which Tommy Hilfiger's daughter and her best friend want to start a charity to give the poor used mattresses, and *Sorority Life*, where producers got a bunch of random co-eds to rush the only sorority at UC Davis that would agree to be filmed. I watched these shows with fascination as a tween, particularly because, if you are not very familiar with the effects of alcohol, the way that drunk people act is upsetting, confusing, and mysterious.

Despite being tacky artifacts of Bush-era cultural cravenness, these shows do a surprising amount to interrogate the concept of "reality." It is common knowledge that every stilted, mesmerizing minute of *The Hills* was scripted for the cameras, its stars eventually acting out fictional feuds and relationships, their daily lives and experiences no longer having any impact on the direction the story lines took. Even with shows that are less staged, the disturbing fact is that a reality show changes its stars' lives more than their lives change the show. Jason Wahler, who starred on both *Laguna Beach* and *The Hills*, has said that he became an alcoholic on the set of *Laguna Beach*, a show following a group of rich high schoolers in Orange County. He went on *Celebrity Rehab with Dr. Drew* to deal with his addiction five years later, adding a new narrative of "reality" to lay over his real life.

At the start, E!'s short-lived 2010 reality show *Pretty Wild* was a completely generic specimen of the reality soap opera. The show follows two teenage socialites, Alexis Neiers and her sister Tess Taylor. Neiers is baby-faced and vapid, whereas Taylor is a year older, sexier, and more world-weary. The girls are trying to start their modeling careers, dreaming of being in *Playboy* just like their mother, Andrea Arlington-Dunn, had been in the eighties. The show has countless silly reality TV setups: Tess goes on a lackluster "date" with singer Ryan Cabrera, who has been courting girls with reality shows since 2003, when he dated Ashlee Simpson at the time of her MTV series. (He was also one of Audrina Patridge's love interests on *The Hills*.) The girls gamely play up their shallow, ridiculous personas for the camera. Neiers talks about how she is eager to be in the music video for Mickey Avalon's new song "Rock Bitch." "It says in the song, 'sliding down from heaven on a stripper pole,'" she says. "And I was like, 'That's totally me!'"

The family's weirdo factor is their mother's wacky spiritualism. Their house is decorated with three-foot Buddha heads, and Dunn says that she's designed her homeschooling curriculum around *The Secret*. The family prays incessantly, ending each prayer with the affirmative "and so it is" instead of "amen." Dunn is often shown wearing the earclips that go with her "frequency meter." This might have been all the show was: *Playboy,* vodka cranberries, *The Secret*. But three events changed the show's course and its destiny, making it a significant artifact of Hollywood crime history and a testament to the competing realities of "reality," journalism, and film.

The first was the revelation, shortly after the show started

filming in summer 2009, of Neiers's involvement in the Bling
Ring, a group of L.A. teenagers who over less than a year stole
more than $3 million of goods from celebrity homes, including,
fittingly, Audrina Patridge's Hollywood Hills mansion. The
second was Neiers's arrest, in 2010, for possession of heroin,
the yearlong stay in rehab that gave her health and sobriety,
and her admission that during the filming of *Pretty Wild* she
"had an over-$10,000-a-week drug habit," "smoking twenty
80 mg oxys a day" and "doing tons of cocaine." The third
was the film based on the story of the Bling Ring, written and
directed by Sofia Coppola, which bases characters on Neiers,
Taylor, and Dunn. The show forms part of the Bling Ring
story's first draft, and it is a source of documentary evidence
that others telling the story have relied on; Coppola's film
faithfully reenacts long scenes from *Pretty Wild*. But the show
is not a documentary, and especially with Neiers's later revela-
tions, it is interesting particularly for what it invents and leaves
out. Since the Bling Ring has been depicted in so many genres,
the show is a study in reality TV as a form of fiction.

Pretty Wild makes for uncomfortable television: the real
strife in its subjects' lives resists the conventions of staged
reality TV, a form that is placid, awkward, and artificial. At
times the staged scenes spin out of control, as the family's
problems assert themselves unexpectedly. In the last episode
of the series, the producers broach Neiers's addiction lamely,
with scenes of Dunn finding a bottle of Xanax and a sleepy-
looking Neiers walking around holding a blanket. Dunn says
that Neiers has been acting strange "for the past two days."
She must have been aware of Neiers's substance abuse be-

fore then, considering that by Neiers's later account, when the show wasn't filming she was "living at a Best Western on Franklin and Vine" because of her drug habit. During the episode, Taylor, Dunn, and Neiers's younger sister, Gabby, decide to have what they call "a little intervention." But the intervention escalates scarily and unexpectedly. Shortly after their supportive opening comments, the family starts yelling at Neiers, following her as she runs through the house and saying, "You are a drug addict!" and "You are crazy!" "Everyone saw Anna Nicole like this, too," Dunn says to her. "And look at her now." That hits so close to the reality of Neiers's drug problem that I find myself hoping it wasn't in the script.

This slippage between the real and the fake is disorienting and sad. One can imagine that the family might have found comfort in the show's alternate reality. Their enthusiastic participation in this heightened, simplified performance of their lives could explain why the most real moments on the show feel the most false. When the police come to the house to arrest Neiers for her involvement in the Bling Ring, Gabby appears at the top of the stairs and yells theatrically, "What is going on?" Her performance is so phony that you could assume the cameras missed the actual moment of the arrest and the show's producers have reenacted it. But then the police officer at the door says, "Shut off the cameras," and the picture goes dark. So the scene couldn't have been staged. Could it?

The immortal moment in *Pretty Wild* occurs after Neiers has agreed to be interviewed by *Vanity Fair* reporter Nancy

Jo Sales. Neiers is devastated by "lies" Sales writes about her, including that she wore six-inch Christian Louboutin heels to court, when in fact she was wearing "four-inch little brown Bebe shoes." Neiers is shown in hysterics, recording voice mail after tearful voice mail for Sales. On the show we see a portion of their interview, and it is so chummy that Sales's ultimate betrayal does feel a little unseemly. "We are so wholesome and down-to-earth," Neiers says, lounging with Sales on a bed. When Neiers breaks down, talking about the "very rocky, tough, tough times" in her life, Sales gives her a hug. This is the predicament of the journalist that Janet Malcolm famously talks about in *The Journalist and the Murderer*. The journalist promises to tell her subject's story when that is never her intention: Sales is loyal to her own story, not Neiers's. Sales's article also mentions Neiers's use of oxycodone, which is a more logical reason for her meltdown than Sales getting her shoes wrong. This fact is not mentioned on *Pretty Wild*, which of course is not telling the whole story either.

Coppola based *The Bling Ring* on Sales's article, and its dialogue is often pulled directly from it. The most outrageous borrowed lines in the movie come from the character based on Neiers, played by Emma Watson. "I'm a firm believer in karma," Watson says fatuously, "and I think this situation was attracted into my life because it was supposed to be a huge learning lesson for me to grow and expand as a spiritual human being." Watson's contempt for her own character is obvious. "I want to lead a huge charity organization," she says with sticky insincerity. "I want to lead a country for all I know."

Coppola gave actual words spoken by Neiers to a classy British actress to say in an over-the-top Valley girl accent, so that the fakeness of the delivery heightens the reality and ridiculousness of the lines, making the obvious point of the film even more obvious: these kids are shitheads. But as closely as the film re-created things Neiers really said, Watson's portrayal of her is different from Neiers's character on *Pretty Wild*. On the show, Neiers is babyish, silly, and mannered—she comes downstairs the day after she's arrested wearing a pair of pink short shorts with POLE HOTTIE printed on the butt—but she is not the cold, robotic, empty-headed beauty queen of the movie. She is at times blindly affectionate toward her sisters, at other times hysterical and desperate, understandable when considering the severity of her addiction and the long prison sentence she was facing for her involvement in the robberies.

Coppola's film allows the audience to enjoy the audacity with which the Bling Ring fulfilled their fantasy of owning a piece of celebrity, while it comfortably condemns them as stupid, entitled, and amoral. They almost certainly were these things. But *Pretty Wild*, despite all of its artificiality, sometimes gets closer to the real story by acknowledging a truth *The Bling Ring* doesn't deal with: shitheads have feelings, too.

Throughout *Pretty Wild*'s nine episodes, Neiers frequently bursts into a litany of her good attributes. "I'm a great person," she says. "And people who really know me, who did do their research on me, would know the great things I do for the community, for this universe." "We are successful, independent, strong women," she and Taylor tell each other on the beach in Cabo. "My main destiny in life is to be a leader," Neiers tells Sales during their interview, and later, when she is leaving her a voice mail, she says, sobbing, "I opened up to you so the world could potentially know what a great, amazing, strong, talented, healthy girl I am."

Coppola has interpreted this habit basically as a kind of PR damage control, Neiers's clumsy attempt to shape her public image. But *Pretty Wild* offers another explanation. The beliefs that Neiers was raised with, essentially the self-help spirituality of *The Secret* and Ernest Holmes's Religious Science movement, place a huge emphasis on the power of positive thinking. Neiers learned from a young age that she could control her reality with this compulsive affirmation. "If Buddha can sit under a tree for forty days, I can do this," Neiers says after she is sentenced to six months in jail. "I can do this."

Neiers, her sisters, and her mom are a close, indulgent family, saying, "I'm so proud of you" at the smallest signs of progress. Their cheery approach to their problems is ultimately what makes *Pretty Wild* so sad. Dunn talks about how she hasn't been able to establish boundaries with her children. She walks in on Taylor in the shower and says, "Nobody has breasts like you do," then enlists Gabby to help with an impromptu nude photo shoot. At one point, Dunn tearfully apologizes for not being a good role model and not setting rules for the girls. "Yeah, we've been crazy and wild,"

Neiers says to comfort her. "But we love each other." This is obviously true, but it couldn't prevent Neiers from going to jail, and it couldn't prevent her addiction.

The proof of Neiers's sincerity on *Pretty Wild* is how similar she sounds now, when she is sober, an adult, a wife, and a mother. Her message is still close to the one Watson repeated in *The Bling Ring*, that her hardships were all for the best. "I believe that in some weird way, this whole thing with the Bling Ring, this whole reality show, is going to give me an opportunity to help people," she said recently in an interview. It seems like the spiritualism she was raised with has dovetailed with the rhetoric of addiction and recovery. Recovery places an emphasis on honesty, stripping away the layers of deception that build up in an addiction, but this honesty is also a pose, just like the positive thinking of Neiers's childhood. Like all systems of self-improvement, it's a way to fake it until you make it.

Even today, Neiers denies any responsibility for the Bling Ring burglaries. Despite the fact that other members of the group have talked about her participation, and she is shown on a surveillance video leaving Orlando Bloom's mansion, and items stolen from celebrities were found at her home, she insists that she sat in a parked car outside Bloom's house, "totally loaded," while the others committed the burglary, and she "never stepped foot in that house." "I gladly share my deepest and darkest secrets to the world in the hopes of helping others with my story," she said. "Why wouldn't I admit to stealing to support my drug habit?" But as we have seen, there are so many motives, so many complications: Neiers's reality doesn't have to be the real story. I suppose the truth exists in some combination of all the ways the Bling Ring has been documented and interpreted, a symphony of stories in which each lets some things go conveniently unsaid. The shows, articles, books, movies, police reports, interviews, and confessions hum it together in the low moments: what really happened and why.

My Hypochondria

I caught hypochondria mysteriously at the age of twenty-two, a few months before I learned my father was in congestive heart failure, which was a few months before my mother had surgery to replace a leaking valve in her heart. I see them as conveniently related, my parents' crises and my long season of terror about cancer, HIV, Lyme, and flesh-eating bacteria, but that cause and effect is faulty—not only did my anxiety start before my parents got sick, it was more likely chemical, the tapered end of a yearlong withdrawal from the antidepressants I'd taken for nine years. I've come to think of my hypochondria more as an extreme of self-obsession. Worries for my family's health barely entered into it; in fact, my hypochondria helped distract me.

My hypochondria made me feel special, like I had come to the ultimate insight: that I one day would die. There was no arguing with the logic of my fears, as in all likelihood I would get sick, though there was no telling when. But it was strange how at the same time that I thought I was being realistic and facing my own mortality, I engaged in a new kind of magical thinking. Rather than believe the world was truly indifferent to me, I believed that I had become the target of all of its bad luck. There are exceptions delineated in every WebMD article I've read. Infections can be impervious to antibiotics. You could be pregnant even if you've gotten your period. Almost anything can be a symptom for Lyme. These exceptions spoke to me and about me in the late-night glow of my laptop screen. Once as I was driving Highway 60 toward Los Angeles, I saw the familiar sign for the carpool lane, HOV 2+, and it momentarily transformed itself into a diagnosis: HIV+. Embarrassingly, I took this as an omen. This was truly stupid, confronting the universe's randomness by doubling down on my belief that I was its protagonist. I compromised by allowing the story to be a tragedy.

The main character in Agnès Varda's 1962 New Wave classic *Cléo from 5 to 7* seeks bad omens, too. A pop star who is remarkable for her vanity and childishness, Cléo spends the day the film documents in agony, waiting for test results that will tell her whether her stomach illness is something serious. The first scene shows Cléo visiting a psychic for a tarot reading, one that presages evil forces, illness, and even death. "The cards said I was sick," Cléo sobs to her assistant after the reading. "Is it written on my face?" She meets a young soldier in a park, and he tells her that it's the first day of summer. "It's the longest day of the year," he says. "Today the sun leaves Gemini for Cancer." "Shut your mouth," Cléo says. Varda shows hypochondria as a perfect twentieth-century ailment: terror that is in the end just another decadence.

In my hypochondria, I watched *Cléo from 5 to 7* and I saw myself reflected on-screen—or rather, refracted. At one point Cléo watches a silent short featuring French New Wave superstars Jean-Luc Godard, Anna Karina, Eddie Constantine, and Jean-Claude Brialy. Godard plays a man who watches his lover, Karina, walk down a flight of stairs and trip on a hose. When Godard wears his signature dark glasses, Karina's situation turns dark—she dies and is taken away by a hearse. When he removes them, the hearse transforms to an ambulance, and she is fine. *Cléo from 5 to 7* posits that modern life's endless, mindless watching directs the self inward, rather than outward. Cléo watches the film like she is looking in a mirror.

The meta-joke of these New Wave filmmakers in the film within a film adds to Varda's portrait of the spectacle's concentric rings of self-absorption—not only is *Cléo* a document of its main character's narcissism, but as a movie about a pop singer, it is pop culture regarding itself. Varda shows everything that distracts from the mirror's feedback loop as an unwelcome intrusion. In one scene, Cléo tries on hats, blissfully taking in her face in many mirrors, thinking, "Everything suits me. Trying things on intoxicates me." Then the camera moves outside, and the cars and passersby on the street are reflected in the window of the hat shop. Traffic sounds drown out the scene's romantic music as the real world is superimposed on Cléo's fantasy world.

If *Cléo from 5 to 7* were purely a critique of capitalistic frivolity—*Women trying on hats, disgusting!*—I don't think it would move me. But it's about narcissism as a confused response to an uncertain world: narcissism as political paralysis. After shopping for hats, Cléo listens with dread to a news dispatch on the radio about the singer Édith Piaf recovering from an operation. But other news items hint at the specter haunting the film, the greatest proof in mid-century France that the world is neither good nor predictable: the Algerian War.

Cléo from 5 to 7 was released in April 1962, a month after a cease-fire was declared between French troops in Algeria and the National Liberation Front insurgents, and just two months before Algeria was declared independent. The Algerian War exemplified a particular type of modern war: one waged against communist or Muslim insurgencies; one which resists the use of the word *war* (in Algeria, the term of choice was *pacification*); one marked by the use of terrorism and torture; one in which victory is impossible, and anyway, beside the point. Anyone alive in the twenty-first century knows that this kind of warfare gnaws at the liberal Western conscience and undermines the security wealthy countries believe they have earned.

Hypochondria turns out to be the perfect outlet for societal dread. In Susan Sontag's book-length essays *Illness as Metaphor* and *AIDS and Its Metaphors,* she outlines the ways that mass anxiety has mapped itself onto illness, particularly in modernity. Tuberculosis, which could be transmitted through the air, amplified nineteenth-century fears of pollution and urban filth, just as, post–World War II, metaphors used to explain cancer directly reflected concerns about the age of radiation. As Sontag writes, "Cancer proceeds by a science-fiction scenario: an invasion of 'alien' or 'mutant' cells." Similarly, the sources of moral decay metaphorized as the disease—the unwholesome effects of racism or rock and roll as "cancers" on society—were seen as products of mysterious invasions, dangers catalyzing spontaneously in virtuous American institutions.

AIDS arrived right on time to take advantage of Cold War paranoia about societal infiltration. Sontag quotes from literature on AIDS describing infected cells that "harbor the virus, vulnerable at any time to a final, all-out attack." This image of AIDS as the enemy within is a metaphor for the kind of war Cléo's Paris knew, and the contemporary United States does, too: one of ever-looming threat, sleeper cells, terrorists, and guerrillas, where the difference between you and your enemy is ideological and thus invisible. Information distributed about the threat of AIDS also reinforced how people should think about their endless war. Much of social programming is an education in fear, and, as Sontag writes simply, "Illness is such a perfect repository for people's most general fears about the future."

I was a junior in college and a political science major during the thick of the Iraq War, a year and a half after the news of Abu Ghraib broke. That's when I took a history class about twentieth-century Algeria. We read *The Stranger* and Henri Alleg's precise descriptions of France's campaign of torture there. My reaction to these echoing atrocities was mostly embarrassment. I became fixated on a stupid remark I made in class, so I skipped the rest of the semester. For good measure, I stopped going to all of my other classes, too. I went to the campus every day but spent my time buying expensive foreign fashion magazines at the university bookstore. My backpack was so stuffed with *Vogue*s that there was no room for books. I guess I understood escapism, though I studied hard, dutifully reading each issue from cover to cover. I was through with political science after that, but I didn't admit it right away. In a literal way, it was too depressing.

My junior year of college was the worst relapse of my mental illness since the breaking point the summer of my thirteenth birthday when I stopped sleeping and messianically predicted my own death. That was in August 2001, and my crisis would diffuse to a more sustainable depression for the rest of the fall and winter—for me, and it turned out, for the rest of America. Although my visions of airplanes crashing through the windows of my French class didn't help anything, my anxiety even then defied cause and effect, always early to the party.

More than once I have been surprised to discover that personal tragedy is tinged with some true and mysterious relief. When my father got sick, he and my entire family were visiting me in Montana to celebrate my master's graduation. He had been struggling to breathe but called it "allergies." The morning after the blowout party celebrating my thesis where he and I had matched shots of Jägermeister, my brother's boyfriend saw him in the hotel parking lot doubled over and wheezing and took him to the emergency room.

There was so much terror with the heart disease diagnosis

and for months afterward. Doctors told us what he couldn't do—eat salt, drink alcohol—and at the same time grimly assured us that no matter what, his dangerous irregular heartbeat would return. He had to leave Montana wearing a defibrillator that looked like bombs strapped to his chest. But I also found that my feelings at the time were not at all what I had anticipated. My sadness and fatigue were solid, so different from fear. I slept in the same bed as my mom, in a hotel room in Missoula, and I thought about basically nothing. And once the bad thing was a reality, my brain began, inevitably, to deal. Emergency had nothing in common with anxiety because my fears couldn't imagine my survival. Not to mention that my father having heart disease—he rode his bike ten miles a day—was not something I had even had the foresight to be afraid of.

I had these insights about the futility of fear, and still that summer my hypochondria was the worst it has ever been. I was suffused by sexual shame, taking multiple useless pregnancy tests and convincing myself I had genital warts and candida of the throat. I was racked by my phantom problems, indifferent to my parents. When I think of the summer my dad got sick, I barely remember anything about him. Maybe this was grief and brain chemistry, too, but when I consider this reaction, I feel only shame.

It is obvious to me now that I should have read *Illness as Metaphor* and *AIDS and Its Metaphors* in the thick of my hypochondria, which lasted for about four years. Sontag wrote them to "alleviate unnecessary suffering" when people thought about illness, "to calm the imagination, not to incite it." It was in fact my noisy imagination that kept me from reading them. I shuddered at the cover of *AIDS and Its Metaphors*, an abstracted photo of cells under a microscope, a cursed image if I had ever seen one. I was the kind of hypochondriac who avoided the doctor, terrified of the certainty of diagnosis. I wallowed in my fear, prolonging agony that could have been ended by a series of tests.

Sontag writes about the connection between the modern conception of illness and the origins of individualism, with romanticized diseases like TB becoming "an interior décor of the body." This is the lineage of our aestheticizing of mental illness, which is often portrayed as a tragic eccentricity or a surplus of insight: think *The Bell Jar, Girl: Interrupted, A Beautiful Mind*, and our suicided geniuses from Vincent van Gogh to Kurt Cobain. Throughout my childhood and adolescence I was tortured by insomnia and compulsive thinking, but I was satisfied that my misery made me, at the very least, special, and it was possible that it made me brilliant. In reality, the amorphous symptoms that constitute mental illness make it maybe the most common chronic ailment. Sontag's thesis is that our societal metaphors are often sicker than our sicknesses. Her demystification of illness was at odds with my conception of myself, in that it might have led me to get the help I needed.

I hesitate when I associate my hypochondria with narcissism. I don't think an anxiety disorder is a moral defect. But in my hypochondria I was consumed with observing myself—taking my temperature, pressing my lymph nodes, and staring at my teeth in the mirror, like the first Narcissus at the pond. I was confused above all about where my self was and what constituted it, convinced my body concealed both poisonous defects and unseeable beauty. I was young and always randomly heartbroken, and my fears of STDs and cancer were transparently metaphorical: I was afraid of a change to my body that would usurp my identity and render me unlovable, or that a diagnosis would confirm that I was already unlovable.

Part of the problem is that mental illnesses are not primarily bad feelings, but the thought patterns and compulsions the sufferer develops to deal with them. These are difficult to let go of because, in a limited way, they work. Systems of magical thinking do provide reassurance, even if it takes torturous negotiations with one's own brain to get there. I sort of agree with Freud that our mental dysfunctions are related to childhood shame, but rather than repressing shameful parts of ourselves, these dysfunctions help us protect them. As a kid I longed to have glasses, braces, a wheelchair, or a chronic disease, seeing them, heartlessly, as sources of importance and attention. As an adult, my hypochondria both allowed me to indulge that gruesome part of myself and to hate myself for it. I'm afraid of poetic justice finding that morbid child, of the fate of someone who likes pain, but hates punishment.

Sontag's essays are masterpieces of compassion. When she probes our "punitive or sentimental fantasies" about sickness, she reveals how cruel they are to the sick. Of course, when confronted directly about my fear, I would have denied that a sick person is unlovable, or less himself or herself, or less human. But even then I knew the stigmas my fears played on were cruel. I could analyze my dark thoughts, but I wouldn't let go of them. Eula Biss writes in *On Immunity*, a kind of successor to Sontag's essays, that "as with other strongly held beliefs, our fears are dear to us." And our fantasies of ourselves are dear to us, and they can make us monstrous.

In the years since my hypochondriac era, I have found that narcissism is anathema to real self-love, which requires forfeiting romantic and morbid notions of identity. I have had to acknowledge that my inner self shares in specialness, rather than possessing its own, and to my surprise, this has expanded my idea of who I am and what I am capable of. "We must have patience with everyone, but especially with ourselves," St. Francis de Sales said, and my practice of self-love is much more a refusal to be cruel to myself than it is any pride or confidence: a reprieve rather than a reward.

The viewer of *Cléo from 5 to 7* is meant to uncomfortably identify with Cléo; she is a sympathetic figure, but not an attractive one. Signs of violence and devastation surround her, but her terror manifests itself as self-absorption. Only when Cléo can truly accept the scale of horror and destruction in the world is she able to free herself from some anxiety. Antoine, the soldier she meets late in the film, is on leave from Algeria, a visitor from the heart of danger. He breaks Cléo's isolation and movingly helps her on her journey to find peace in the universe's indifference. "I'm afraid of everything," Cléo tells him.

"Birds, storms, elevators, needles, and now this great fear of death." "In Algeria, you'd be afraid all the time," Antoine says.

In the long, difficult recovery period after my mom's heart surgery, my brothers and I rushed to my parents' side, spending over a month making messes in their house and providing minimal practical help. One Sunday morning, a few weeks after I came back, I woke to what sounded like an explosion. Outside, we found that a woman had crashed her car into the side of the house, her front bumper landing perilously close to where my mom sat in bed, watching *The Sopranos*. The woman came out of her car lucid, saying she didn't remember the crash and she didn't know what had happened, having blacked out while driving to the church a block away. She came into our house to call her husband, but inside she started seizing, rigid and unresponsive in a chair in our living room.

I called the police, panicked. I didn't know how to tell if she was breathing, didn't know CPR. My nineteen-year-old brother sobbed after the ambulance arrived, asking if she was going to die. As the EMTs worked on her, I went to the church to find her husband. I asked a middle-school-aged usher where he was, then burst in on a meeting of church elders in a conference room. He looked stricken the moment I said her name. He came with me and knelt down and prayed in our driveway. The EMTs administered CPR for a terrifyingly long time, and as they were rushing her to the hospital, we heard someone say that she had responded. When my dad came home from grocery shopping, they had already left. He had missed the whole thing, and he was so innocent of the experience that we were mad at him. The woman didn't die in our house, and she didn't die in the hospital. My mom has seen her since. She lived down the street.

This was another thing I had never thought to be afraid of, and isn't that the way it goes? Disaster finds us, crashes into the side of the house if it has to. As I pondered the freaky randomness of the universe, from which tragedy grows—why our house, of all houses?—I discovered that grace grows there, too, and only there. My family agreed we were thankful that she had run into our house because we had been there and were able to help her. As I threw my winter coat over my pajama pants and sprinted up the street to the church, for once I trusted my body to be enough, to know what to do.

Just Us Girls

John Fawcett's 2000 werewolf film *Ginger Snaps* centers on two spooky teenage sisters, Brigitte and Ginger Fitzgerald, one of whom is bitten by a mysterious fanged beast. It is in the film's first act, after Ginger begins to exhibit strange symptoms—hair growing from the wounds where the creature scratched her, the world's heaviest period, and a newfound interest in boys and marijuana—that it happens: the moment.

The girls' conventional mother, bedecked in a holiday sweat shirt with two bizarre pin curls framing her face, finds Ginger's bloodstained underwear in the dirty laundry. (We have already heard that neither Ginger nor Brigitte has begun menstruating.) Pamela looks at the underwear for a moment, frowns, pauses, and then sprays it vigorously with bleach. Cut to Ginger, Brigitte, and their father sitting at the dinner table. Pamela enters, singsonging "Ginger's very favorite," holding an angel food Bundt cake topped with strawberries. She places the cake in front of Ginger and says, "Congratulations, sweetie," as strawberry sauce oozes luridly down the cake's sides.

This. This. The period cake. The vivid evocation of menstrual blood at a suburban dinner table is so audacious and subversive and gross that you begin to suspect you are not watching just any low-budget Canadian teen gore-fest. You might be sharing in the glory of the greatest werewolf and menstruation-themed feminist horror movie of all time.

I first watched *Ginger Snaps* in the fall after I graduated from college, at the giant old house the manager at the ice cream store where I worked shared with a half-dozen other people. My best friend, B, and I crowded together on their collapsing brown couch and shared one Miller Lite between us. In the following weeks, as fall drew ever wetter and darker, we rented it at a little video store off the highway and watched it again. B had been talked into living in a one-bedroom apartment with a strange girl we knew from college, who at the age of twenty-two did not have a checking account and kept "everything precious to her" in a giant travel trunk that she treated like a pet. I never learned what was in it, but we enjoyed placing our coffee mugs and feet on it when she wasn't around. I saw B's apartment and her roommate as a burden primarily for me, even though the window in B's tiny bedroom was broken and she nearly froze that Nebraska winter.

I would go to B's apartment at ten at night, battle-worn after shifts at the ice cream store, with my bruised forearms crusted with chocolate and my sweat smelling like waffle cone mix. She would microwave me a bowl of canned ravioli she bought especially for me, and we would watch movies in the footprint of her roommate's Murphy bed. After the encore showing of *Ginger Snaps*, we rented *Ginger Snaps 2: Unleashed* and *Ginger Snaps Back: The Beginning*. (The latter is a prequel that follows the sisters' ancestors on the Canadian frontier.) That winter we decorated my apartment with a giant *Ginger Snaps* poster and a *Ginger Snaps* light switch plate that I bought online.

Part of *Ginger Snaps*'s brilliance is that all it aspires to be is a cheesy horror film. Fawcett set out to make a B movie, rejecting CGI and other big-budget effects, so that the actor playing Ginger had to spend hours being outfitted with fangs, cosmetic contact lenses, and even a full facial prosthetic that, according to Wikipedia, "gave her a permanently runny nose that she had to stop up with Q-tips." *Ginger Snaps* creates meaning in the same way as its B-movie fellows, through the strict use of metaphor. In *Ginger Snaps,* we see all that is terrifying about puberty made gruesomely manifest. In puberty, a teenager's body grows and changes in ways that can be painful and grotesque. At the same time, hormones hijack the teenager's emotions, making her behavior more passionate and impulsive. With these fluctuations and transfigurations, the person in the mirror can appear as something terribly other: a hairy monster. And the cycle of menstruation aligns felicitously with the werewolf myth, as both involve, at least in our imaginations, a monthly change into something different, unpredictable, even frightful.

Ginger's transformation begins slowly at first. She has a nightmarish first period and dogs won't stop barking at her. But then her body changes in more alarming ways. A claw protrudes from her ankle and she grows a long, muscular tail. She develops fangs, and her face and torso become gradually more canine until, at the end, she has no human qualities. She is nothing but a giant, snarling, teenage were-wolf. Along the way, she becomes more aggressive, sexually and otherwise. "I get this ache," she says after she loses her virginity. "I thought it was for sex, but it's to tear everything to fucking pieces."

It turns out the emotions and circumstances of puberty elide with those of metamorphosing into a werewolf with remarkable consistency. Ginger's budding sex life threat-ens the close relationship she and Brigitte have always had. "You're doing drugs with guys," Brigitte says. "Something's definitely wrong with you." For Brigitte, this evidence, more than Ginger's fangs or her tail or her bloodlust, proves that something alien is taking over her sister. "Something's wrong with you," Brigitte insists again. "And more than you being just . . . female."

But beyond this outsize metaphor, the more subtle dynamics of jealousy and dependence propel the film's plot. The first time we encounter Brigitte and Ginger, they are staging their own deaths with zeal and creativity, exploring a variety of possible scenarios: Ginger eviscerated by a lawn mower, Brigitte with a pitchfork through her neck, both sisters sipping poison at a tea party, Ginger skewered on a white picket fence. They have made a pact, sealed with blood, to commit suicide before they turn sixteen. "Out by sixteen or dead in the scene, but together forever," they repeat, "united against life as we know it." But Brigitte betrays some hesitation even in these opening scenes. "Don't you think our deaths should be a little more than cheap entertainment?" she asks, worried even then that they might not be rebelling, but rather surrendering to a mainstream culture that adores Dead Girls, the more gruesome, the better. Ginger rejects any worries that dying in this way might be too sensational or dramatic. "Suicide's like the ultimate 'fuck you,'" she says. "It's so us." Ginger is the older sister, and she often defines them as a single individual, taking the liberty to decide what they are.

In the end, Ginger's change reveals how monstrous the girls' relationship is. When her transformation is nearly complete, after she's murdered and infected and terrorized the citizens of their little Canadian town, she pressures Brigitte to become a werewolf also. "It's so us," Ginger tells her. "I'd rather be dead than be what you are," Brigitte says. But Ginger's grotesqueness isn't enough to break what binds them. Eventually Brigitte slits her and Ginger's palms and infects herself. Brigitte believes she has found a cure for lycanthropy, but it also seems that abandoning Ginger is more than she can bear, because she has no identity without her. As she becomes a werewolf herself, Brigitte tells Ginger, "You wreck anything that isn't about you. Now I am you." Their claustrophobic, incestuous bond is a reminder that relationships can be too close, that destruction can yoke two people as well as love can.

I had never enjoyed a horror film before I saw *Ginger Snaps*. It was unclear to me then why I was so immediately obsessed with it, but it makes more sense to me now. I went to college when I was sixteen and graduated when I was nineteen, the entire time feeling like I was in purgatory: from my perspective no one around me was doing much to make the most of their college years either. This was part of a fundamental misunderstanding that sprung from my limited social circle. I insisted that the age difference with my classmates was not the source of my misery, because in my classes I felt no different than anyone else. But the only people who would hang around with me outside of class were do-gooder virgins who would rather make asinine mischief like going to Kmart and buying a bunch of bouncy balls than get wasted. I was often disgusted with them, because who likes a club that will have you as a member?

When I met B in my junior year, it was like the universe had mercy on me. We had a friendship that was, in some ways, like looking in a mirror: I know it sounds on the nose, but we have the same birthday. B is two years older, slightly stunted by controlling, fundamentalist parents who took her on conservative Christian pilgrimages to Focus on the Family headquarters in Colorado Springs. We had so much of the same longing: for lives and friends who were cooler, for a freedom we couldn't have because we couldn't picture it. She was silent in all group situations and could make anything that I requested, including drawings, costumes, headdresses, needlepoint, and duct tape purses of any design. She spoke French and played the piano. She was like all seven muses for me, hanging out up on Mount Olympus, quietly and happily creating.

B and I had schemes large and small. We had a plan to become normal after B's twenty-second birthday by learning to drink alcohol. She would cluelessly buy bottles of Popov and cases of Busch Light for parties we had at my apartment, and this scheme worked in a limited way. For one of the parties, we attempted to re-create the period cake from *Ginger Snaps* using a cake mold shaped like a castle. Many of our schemes were centered on how exactly we would get our first boyfriends, considering that the men we knew were awful and they didn't like us anyway. When B finally did start dating a guy she had liked for years, I was completely perplexed. "I always think, I wish I could find a guy like Alice," she told me once, and it had seemed safely improbable that she would. I was still waiting for a guy like her. Our attachment was not sexual, but when I say I loved B, I mean it. And I think love can last forever, but not that kind, not that way.

From this distance, I can't ignore the ways I controlled and manipulated B. We were not only kindred spirits: I was drawn to her because she was someone quiet and passive for me to boss around. Often I felt like I was helping her, giving her opportunities. To get her to stay in Lincoln after college, I had my mom help get her a job. But I would also fly off the handle at our slightest disagreement, any indication we were not the mirror images we liked to believe. All the places she chose to live were immense trials for me. I saw it as her being manipulated by other people we knew, talked into moving into the apartment with the Murphy bed by friends who knew her roommate, and later persuaded by her mom to move to a suburban apartment complex with her high school friend far away from my apartment. I gave her the silent treatment for days when she moved away from downtown, even though her apartment was only a fifteen-minute drive and had a pool and windows that shut all the way. This should indicate the amount of daily attention I required from her.

In our senior year of college we went to New York on spring break, and I planned our trip down to the minute without any input from B. I created the geekiest and most eccentric itinerary imaginable, not including any partying whatsoever. I took us to see the Chieftains at Carnegie Hall on St. Patrick's Day, a matinee in the very short run of the Broadway musical based on John Waters's film *Cry-Baby*, and a *Flight of the Conchords* walking tour of Lower Manhattan based on my own research. I remember a particularly long and hangry journey deep into Brooklyn to get an inexpensive breakfast I had read about on the Internet, the insane amount we spent on subway fare neutralizing any savings from the cheap diner. It was exhausting to run the show, and I'm sure it was exhausting following along. The next year I went to New York again by myself to visit my aunt and uncle, and I spent most of the time in their apartment watching the first season of *RuPaul's Drag Race*. By then the handwriting was on the wall: as often as I nursed feelings of betrayal and abandonment toward B, of course I was the one who left her.

The horror in *Ginger Snaps* comes from codependence taken to its extreme of dysfunction, an extreme B and I maybe should have treated as a cautionary tale. But Brigitte and Ginger's personal dysfunction points to broader societal dysfunctions, to narratives and expectations that push women and girls to exhaustion, to sickness. Their mother does everything she can to be a perfect suburban housewife—cooking, cleaning, and crafting, encouraging and caring for her daughters in spite of their weirdness—and by the end is cracking in her archetype. When she discovers that the girls have killed a popular girl who tormented them, she suggests they just start over. "First thing tomorrow, I'll let the house fill up with gas and I'll light a match. We'll start fresh," she says. "Just us girls."

"Just us girls" is a succinct description of Brigitte and Ginger's ethos. Their attitudes are at times misogynistic ("Wrists are for girls," Ginger says when contemplating methods of suicide), but really what they long for is an all-female world. Since they know that puberty and the development of their sexuality may eventually lead them to need men, even want them, they see only one solution: to develop relationships only with each other and die before they reach adulthood.

We can look to a number of cultural forebears of the Fitzgerald sisters—the heroines of Jeffrey Eugenides's novel *The Virgin Suicides* are also familiar with the calamity that sexual maturity can pose. *Hamlet*'s Ophelia retreats intentionally into madness as her only recourse to express her grief, and turns to suicide when all the male figures in her life have failed her. There is also the uncanny matriarch of American poetry, about whom a *VICE* headline once said, "Emily Dickinson Was Horny and Ready to Die." *Ginger Snaps* is, then, a very old story: the feminine descent into insanity, into wildness, into what is morbid, dark, odd, and scary. As Anne Carson delineates in her essential essay "The Gender of Sound," Aristotle associates femaleness with all that is "curving, dark, secret, evil, ever-moving, not self-

contained, and lacking its own boundaries." Describing an
ancient Greek poem in which a man who is far from home
can hear the sounds of both wolves and women howling, she
writes,

> The wolf is a conventional symbol of marginality
> in Greek poetry . . . He lives beyond the bound-
> ary of usefully cultivated and inhabited space . . .
> Women, in the ancient view, share this territory
> spiritually and metaphorically in virtue of a "nat-
> ural" female affinity for all that is raw, formless,
> and in need of the civilizing hand of man.

In light of women's problematic and long-standing affilia-
tion with wolves, a werewolf movie involving pubescent girls
feels less cheesy and more truly serious all the time.

It seems that one outcome of the feminine being's "lacking
its own boundaries" is that female pain is often collective.
There have been incidents of a kind of "mass hysteria" in
the very recent past: in 1962 a so-called laughter epidemic
began with three high school girls in the Tanzanian village
of Kashasha and eventually affected several villages and one
thousand people. In an Upstate New York high school in
early 2012, fifteen girls, many of them cheerleaders, started
displaying Tourette's syndrome–like symptoms. Girls charge
one another with their suffering, and they take up the pa-
thologies of their friends and sisters, in an interlocking web
of cruelty and solidarity.

Carson writes how Sigmund Freud coined the term *hys-*

teria to describe "female patients whose tics and neuralgias and convulsions and paralyses and eating disorders and spells of blindness could be read, in his theory, as a direct translation into somatic terms of psychic events upon the woman's body." In *Ginger Snaps*, emotional pain is manifest on the Fitzgerald sisters' bodies, even before their encounter with the werewolf. In Freud's conception, their hysterical behavior was the only way for women to express what was going on in their minds. Hysteria was a rupture rooted deep in the subconscious, a terrible secret unearthed, "as if the entire female gender," Carson writes, "were a kind of collective bad memory of unspeakable things."

And yet all of these common female performances—as someone proper, chaste, and controllable; a wolflike other; or a hysterical invalid—are conceived of and defined by the patriarchy. Carson speaks of how *Playboy* magazine will print interviews with famous feminists alongside nude centerfold pictorials. "Each of them," she writes, "the centerfold naked woman and the feminist, a social construct purchased and marketed by *Playboy* magazine to facilitate that fantasy of masculine virtue." Brigitte and Ginger, in their transgressions and their transformations, are still participating in a narrative authored and perpetuated by a society that desires for girls to be wild, perverse, and "in need of the civilizing hand of man."

I am attempting to avoid these traps sprung in the narratives of female experience, like I'm winding my way through some sort of feminist labyrinth—how do you think I'm doing? When I moved to Montana for graduate school, B and I talked on the phone constantly, but circumstances conspired to change our relationship. She came to visit me in the spring in Montana, not asking before she booked a trip for a full seven days. I was weirdly itchy about this collision of my old and new lives, and even though B would go off on her own for hours at a time, her presence still made me cranky. I felt like a kid who regrets asking her friend to sleep over. We were still best friends, but she wasn't my one and only. Still, I consider our friendship a kind of twinning, embracing all the erotic potential of that phrase. Intimate best friendships are the first committed relationships many American girls have, and whether they are sexual or not, they are romantic. Girls give each other presents, cuddle and kiss each other, braid each other's hair and do each other's makeup, talk for hours on the phone, write each other notes covered in hearts, say "I love you" and mean it.

At times it felt like B and I kept each other girls too long, like Ginger trying to keep Brigitte forever sixteen. I am tempted to say that B and I had to change our relationship in order to grow up, but "grow up" contains so many hetero-normative expectations, including the one that primary relationships must be the kind that could lead to marriage, kids, and a retirement plan. Sisterhood has been one of the foremost queering forces in Western culture, including in particular the professional sisterhood of the convent. There is also the venerable tradition of spinsterism, and pairs of spinster sisters have been immortalized over and over, from the murderous old ladies in *Arsenic and Old Lace* to the saintly ones in *Babette's Feast*.

True, female relationships are often fraught, untenable, and toxic, maybe because they're expected to be that way. Think of Peter Jackson's murderous teenage lovers in *Heavenly Creatures* or the secrets and betrayals between Nel and Sula in *Sula*. When girls are cruel and manipulative to their sisters and best friends, when they contract secrets and compulsions and disorders from them, they are acting out another script authored by a sexist society. And it is not only that sisters are expected to share dysfunction, but that our culture encourages female intimacy while also despising women without men and suspecting that they are wild and sinister. This contradiction produces shame and anger in girls, who take out their rage on the only people who are vulnerable to them, by punishing and policing their sisters but also themselves. I recognize this quick-burning, misplaced anger in my relationship with B, which was a kind of closeness where any boundary was a betrayal.

The world Ginger and Brigitte grow up in is truly out of a horror story, where the initiation into womanhood is either a quick, monstrous death sentence or a slow death of the soul. We must try to give female relationships the space they deserve, not treating them as aberrations or cautionary tales, but remembering how Sula becomes Nel's only regret, and how, in the Book of Ruth, Ruth says to Naomi, "Where you go I will go, and where you stay I will stay." Rather than casting my story with B as another case of too-close female friendship, I should probably say that like many first loves, it did not survive the switch to long distance, but thankfully, we stayed friends. When I was twenty, B drew a portrait of

the virgin martyr St. Agnes of Rome and I got it tattooed on
my arm, so that some part of B is mine forever. Agnes was
a pious teenager who died rather than marry one of her rich
suitors, saying of her executioner, "This butcher is the lover
who pleases me." It's that same old story, about a spooky girl
who died for love too young.

Part 4

A Sentimental
Education

Accomplices

The imposition of a sentimental, or false, narrative on the disparate and often random experience that constitutes the life of a city or a country means, necessarily, that much of what happens in that city or country will be rendered illustrative, a series of set pieces, or performance opportunities.

—JOAN DIDION, "SENTIMENTAL JOURNEYS"

Well. Time passes and passes. It passes backward and it passes forward and it carries you along, and no one in the whole wide world knows more about time than this: it is carrying you through an element you do not understand into an element you will not remember. Yet, *something* remembers—it can even be said that something avenges: the trap of our century, and the subject now before us.

—JAMES BALDWIN, *NO NAME IN THE STREET*

1.

For years every essay I wrote started with "I moved to Los Angeles" because it was the only brave or interesting thing I had ever done. Much to my delight, my own biography had converged with one of the perennial themes of modern storytelling: the provincial naïf lost in the big city, learning hard lessons among the urban eccentrics. It's a narrative that is almost universally understandable, and, probably because of that, at least partially a lie. Moving there was difficult. I couldn't find a job, couldn't figure out which directions the streets ran, couldn't keep track of my wallet, and had to order new credit cards and a new driver's license—twice. The lie in this narrative is not false naïveté. I really was that stupid, and I had no right to be.

I moved there a few weeks after I turned twenty-five, as I lost my last, most questionable claims on youth, still never having had a steady relationship or a real job. I had spent my entire life in Idaho, Nebraska, and Montana. I crammed for my new big city life in a Salt Lake City motel room, googling "How do you drive on a freeway?" The summer before I moved to L.A., I drove to my aunt and uncle's house in Chico, California, north of Sacramento, in my battered pink Oldsmobile. I had never been to California, never seen a palm tree or the beach. I was pet-sitting for them as they took a cross-country road trip, despite the fact that I had always been more or less terrified of animals.

Having felt lonely all my life, I was for the first time alone.

That is probably why I quickly became obsessed with my
aunt and uncle's dog, Sweet Pea, a pudgy two-year-old Chi-
huahua mix gnarled by an early life on the streets, who was,
nevertheless, beautiful. I had never walked, fed, or bathed
a dog, and rarely had I taken pleasure in petting one, but I
would hold Sweet Pea from when I read mystery novels in
the morning to when I watched *Dateline* at night. At times
she would wriggle from my lap and lie on the floor to escape
my constant hugging. We were together so much that I found
myself, unsettlingly, thinking of her less as a pet and more as
a roommate. At the Safeway, wondering if we were low on
dog food, I thought, *I'll text Sweet Pea.*

Being so newly alone, I ended up doing strange things.
I went to karaoke at a random bar and, before I sang, announced that I was new in town and had no friends. I was
quickly adopted by a set of sweet, hip townies a few years
younger than I was. At the same bar on another night I met
the man I started sleeping with. He was thirty-three, a former cop who had been wounded on the force, got fired, sued
the city, and used his settlement to go back to college. In
movie voice-over terms: I learned a lot that summer. I felt free
to have experiences I had only heard of—"casual dating,"
"dogsitting," "meeting new people"—once I was living in a
place where absolutely no one cared what I did. But it is dangerous to grow up so late. Desperately bored, I drove nearly
two hours to Davis one night to watch *The Bling Ring.* Coming back home through Sacramento, I missed my freeway
exit three times. Each time I got off on the next one, circled
around, got back on the freeway, and drove right past it. It

did not occur to me until I was surrounded by cars speeding through an unfamiliar city: *Ah*, I thought, with some wonder, *I need glasses*.

It was a summer of road trips. I drove my 1995 Oldsmobile thousands of miles up remote mountain roads in the Sierra Nevadas and down through the Grapevine to Hollywood. I loved and trusted my car completely, believing it to be low maintenance, resilient, and perfectly behaved in all weather. As I took one last trip, north through the Cascades on the way to Portland, in a scorching August on the hottest stretch of I-5, the car began to overheat. I was spacing out slightly when a light on my dashboard began to flash. Then more lights started flashing, and a loud dinging shook through my skull. It took me a while to figure out what was going on, as I was unable to read the familiar symbols on my dashboard. I rejected the only obvious response—pull the car over—and I kept going until the engine made a horrifying crack and my car was good and dead. A person who will keep driving on a busy mountain highway as her car boils over may be an adult, but she has not learned to act like one.

As I write my version of a Hello to All That, I am aware that this story is supposed to be told about New York, not L.A. There are of course books and movies about people moving to Los Angeles, but they are almost always seeking stardom or, more modestly, work in the entertainment industry. I can't think of any documents of a new writer or artist moving to L.A. with no prospects, seeking only misadventurously to "find herself." If you can, please let me know. We are all suckers for these stories of urban acclimatization because they allow for situations that are so adolescent: feeling left out, trying to analyze the clothes and haircuts of cool people, stupid mistakes, electric new experiences, false hope, sharp sadness, and embarrassing attempts at self-reinvention.

That vulnerable mood is the main appeal of Rachel Kushner's art-and-anarchy novel *The Flamethrowers*, at least for me. I read it in my first year in Los Angeles as a newborn *urban* artist, raw to the world. Kushner's novel, probably one of the most celebrated works of fiction of the early twenty-first century, is highly brainy, informed by ideas about time and chaos laid out by the intellectual movements of the 1970s, from land art to the Italian anarchist movement Autonomia Operaia. But the book's tender heart is its vivid heroine and narrator, unnamed but sometimes called Reno, because that's where she's from.

The Flamethrowers documents the narrator's journey to New York in the early seventies as she seeks the vibes of the downtown art scene. She has just finished art school at the University of Nevada at Reno, and she reminisces about her working-class childhood riding on her cousins' motorcycles and ski racing in the Sierra Nevadas. I also grew up in a western backwater and went to a state university, so I immediately loved this book. I recognized so much of my own romance and confusion as she describes her early wonder at the city, the way Fourteenth Street glittered in a tropical light that would disappear once she knew it well. She is alienated from excitement she imagines all around her, her loneliness casting a spell of silence that is sporadically, jarringly broken by odd encounters. She tags along one night with some art-world libertines, an older southern gentleman and his girlfriend, a tragic nymphic beauty. They bullshit about everything, tell her lies and sob stories, make assumptions about her life, ask her questions and don't listen to the answers. Their night climaxes in a hotel room as the narrator watches them slow-dance with a bottle of Cutty Sark and a loaded handgun.

I knew how thankful you could be for inexplicable episodes like this. Even the imperfect friendly gesture can be a mercy, and then you are mercifully free to walk away from whatever bizarre humanity you have witnessed. My first weeks in L.A. I hemorrhaged my birthday money driving insane distances from where I was crashing in Long Beach, eating breakfast alone in Echo Park and going to karaoke alone at midnight in Culver City. Once I was caught in traffic on the 710 for nearly an hour, one of those cliché traffic jams where people get out of their cars and walk around on the freeway. My hosts in Long Beach were my friends from college who had both gotten jobs as train conductors. They would be gone for days at a time and then come back in powerfully bad moods, which they remedied by drinking cases of Bud Light Lime and undertaking schemes like meeting girls from Cal State Fullerton at bars near Disneyland. When their lifestyle became too much for me, I got a cheap hotel room thirty miles north in Alhambra, where I watched MTV and tried to conceive of what the hell I was doing there. I chose the most difficult version of L.A., the one that meant endless arduous journeys by car, so the city was totally accessible to me except any parts of it that might have made sense. This lifestyle was unsustainable, and luckily I didn't have to sustain it for long: when I finally settled in Koreatown, parking was at such a premium that I moved my car only when it was mandated for street cleaning. I walked to the many beloved landmarks near my neighborhood, including the Brass Monkey karaoke bar, Hollywood Forever Cemetery, and the best Oaxacan food in L.A.

"I was in the stream that had moved around me since I'd arrived. It had moved around me and not let me in and suddenly here I was, at this table, plunged into a world, everything moving swiftly but not passing me by," Kushner's narrator says about her night with the people with the gun, describing an experience that is not quite initiation, not inclusion even, but what could be a satisfying substitute. In L.A. I felt this stream move around me on the freeways as I wondered where everyone else was going and if I should be going there, too. There were nights I almost dipped into the stream. Once my cousin Tony, a reality TV producer who was trying to reinvent himself as a comedy writer and stand-up comedian, took me to an IKEA in Burbank with his friend, a much more successful comedian with stoned, bloodshot eyes, and an annoying woman I could never figure out. Was she the comedian's girlfriend? Or also a comedian herself? We were looking for brown fabric to repair a sofa slipcover that the comedian had burned a hole in. This was an important mission because his roommate was very pissed. We smoked weed before we went in and Tony and I walked around looking at pillows.

"What would this place be like during an earthquake?" Tony said.

I looked at all the flimsy merchandise seeming to teeter above our heads.

"I think a lot about earthquakes," Tony said. "But don't worry. Los Angeles is a very earthquake-safe city. I've done the research."

The woman and the comedian made fun of me for never having been to IKEA, like going there made them urban sophisticates. They dropped me home abruptly after we failed to find the fabric because Andy Dick wanted the comedian to come with him to Jumbo's Clown Room, the famous hipster strip club.

I was thankful for the company but ultimately frustrated by this episode, mostly because I thought Tony was a dorky, desperate rube like me, despite the fifteen years he had spent in New York working in TV. A week afterward he sent me a string of seven text messages, which I immediately assumed was bad news about one of our elderly relatives. Instead, it was a story about how the woman we went to IKEA with had propositioned him. He turned her down because he didn't want to step on the comedian's toes—he was too valuable a professional connection. This left me profoundly bummed out about the entertainment industry. Tony avoided every opportunity to waste time, to be bored or embarrassed, to burn a bridge or break a heart, driven only by minute-by-minute calculations about how to advance his career, and he still had nothing to show for it. I thought he was an idiot. I believed that having an experience, even a messy one, was the way to tell the city you belonged.

This belief might also explain why, despite the comfort

of family Tony provided, I didn't really want to be hanging around a guy I was related to. My first six months in Los Angeles were a series of abortive crushes. I was obsessed with my coworker at my restaurant job, a UCLA dropout, probably because he knew what an MFA was. He taught me how to steal whole bags of Intelligentsia coffee beans from work, and I was convinced he was some sort of sociopathic genius. Another time, an old classmate who wrote for a famously maligned sitcom took me to a rooftop biergarten in Echo Park. Remembering how I had liked him in grade school band, I thought he might be my destiny. He sent me wistful text messages every few months after that, but we never hung out again.

These early extremes of hope were a prelude to the false hope frenzy I experienced when, bored of the days where I walked across the street to get pad thai or next door to buy hair ties at the dollar store or down the block to get a burrito from a truck—alone, alone, alone—I signed up for several online dating services. Good first dates led me to desperate sexting and crying in my kitchen. This was a useful if horrifying experience that I won't linger on long. Internet dating confirmed that there were many men who wanted to date me. I had always been told they were out there, and here they were, unmasked. I was also exposed, uncomfortably, to all the men whom I did not want to date. Even as I bathed in the gorgeous sorrow of rejection, which my messy heart found in abundance, I learned to be the one who said no—not only to men I wasn't attracted to but to those who made me feel bad, to those who were bad news. One of the best dates I had was with a hyperactive younger guy, a native Angeleno who told me, dubiously, that he was a fashion designer. We sang karaoke at the Brass Monkey and he kept suggesting we join a sloshy bachelorette party—they just seemed so fun. I stole his hat, a floral Dodgers snapback, as he walked me home. After he left, I impulsively texted him that I expected him to kiss me. He ran back to my door and gave me one perfect rom-com kiss. I told him I would give him his hat back on our next date, but it never happened. I was uncharacteristically tranquil about where things had ended. His hat is now somewhere in Silver Lake, at the home of my ex-boyfriend. This date foreshadowed a plot twist where, contrary to the stories I was used to telling about the character who was myself, I was not the one who got her heart broken.

In *The Flamethrowers*, when the narrator gets to New York, she calls a number she's been given for her college crush, an older art student who paved her way to the city from Reno, but it's been disconnected. A little while later, after a disappointing one-night stand, she calls it again. "It may go without saying that I was the type of person who would call a disconnected number more than once," she says to explain the fantasy she was suspended in. I underlined this three times in my copy of the book. I know the shame in believing something could work out, that there is someone on the other end of the line who is as primed for love as you are: the naïveté the city is supposed to strip from you. But longing is such a pathetically feminine trait, one that we so often hate in ourselves and others. That night in *The Flamethrowers* when the narrator meets the people with the gun, their friend

Ronnie tells her that she moved to New York to fall in love, which she immediately denies. Later, she says this felt like a trap. "I didn't move here not to fall in love," she says. "The desire for love is universal but that has never meant it's worthy of respect. It's not admirable to want love, it just is."

My other favorite Hellos to All That are in the prose of Eileen Myles, the legendary New York poet. I met Myles when she was a visiting professor at my grad school in Montana. Her presence launched our entire program into a semester of manic excitement, even though she was extremely chill, dutifully showing up to every reading and drinking Diet Coke in a corner. My friends who were in her class told me that her highest praise was saying that something was art, or in her Boston accent, *aht*. I've reintroduced myself to her since and she only looked at me painedly, saying finally (for my benefit), "You look familiar."

Myles's wonderful, riffing biographical novels *Inferno* and *Chelsea Girls* depict "Eileen" showing up in New York City at twenty-five wondering if she can become what she secretly is: a poet and a lesbian. The titles *Inferno* and *The Flamethrowers* both recall clichés of initiation: "out of the frying pan and into the fire" or "a trial by fire," figuring New York City as a flaming gauntlet for young women to pass through. With idiosyncratic cool, Myles writes all the mysterious and painful and ecstatic rites of passage Eileen endures in 1970s New York. One night a woman calls her and tells her she got her number from her stepbrother and wonders if Eileen could tell her about "opportunities in the poetry field."

It turns out she is not a writer but a prostitute, and Eileen spends one night working with her, on a "date" with a pair of Italian businessmen. Eileen takes the train to Queens once a month for years to get her speed prescription from a diet doctor, then sells the pills and gives them away to friends at downtown poetry workshops led by New York School poets like Alice Notley and Ted Berrigan. She takes temporary jobs apple picking upstate or dip-dying picture frames in Maine.

Despite the monumental feel of Myles's stories—especially in *Chelsea Girls*, where the chapters' endings are often as brutal and abrupt as the kicker in a comic strip—her out-of-order episodes also evoke life as an undulating journey through a series of more or less similar days. In *Inferno*, she describes an early day in the city:

> Here I was doing my laundry in New York. Watching my rags go round and round. I had escaped. Dogs on Thompson St. were barking, crazy people flying by in and out of the opened doors—a couple having a fight. I was reading a book. Life was like doing your laundry.

This daily rhythm is inextricable from the daily struggle to get and keep work—long-term or temporary, honest or illicit, skilled or menial—that runs through all of Myles's writing. "At 59 I've come to identify myself as working class though kind of middle now," she writes in the first essay in her collection of nonfiction, *The Importance of Being Ice-land*, in her typical off-the-cuff style, which makes much of her prose read like a wonderful, dashed-off email from a friend. "I'm a poet and a novelist, one-time college professor, among other things. Generally as many things as possible." Working-class jobs are marked by grinding or graceful repetitions, and the form of Myles's novels—less a traditional plot arc than a series of oscillating waves—imitates the jobs her family worked: her father was a mailman, her aunt cleaned toilets at Harvard, and Eileen, in *Inferno* and *Chelsea Girls*, works in hotels, department stores, restaurants, bars, and factories. In fact, the practice of poetry seems like the perfect mimesis for the traditional work of the working class, a series of repetitions that pile up and go nowhere, small, inconsequential, and barely remunerative.

It is disarming in her novels how, despite the hepcat quality of her voice, Myles moves so freely between describing the druggy, queer, avant-garde world of seventies and eighties New York and Eileen's conventional working-class Catholic childhood in Boston. These reminiscences serve as the formative experiences traditional to the biography form, but they are also random, nostalgic, and often ugly. Early in *Chelsea Girls*, there is a chapter in which twelve-year-old Eileen watches her father die. She feels her own perversity in the experience, unable to react correctly at the time or in the days after. Lacking the gracious maturity we often ascribe to grieving kids, she feels even younger than she is. "What was I, invisible," she says. "Well, from now on I would be. If they think I am a kid, I will be a kid forever." Thus the tragic origins of her life as an artist, forever playing, skirting respectability—though Myles refuses to connect the dots so cleanly.

At times Myles's books adopt the narrative style of an older relative telling homely, macabre stories about people you've never heard of, like the chapter describing disgraced friends of her parents who both drank themselves to death in one weekend. She explores these humble origins not only to elucidate Eileen's present through her past, but also to set her apart from the rest of the people in her New York scene. She is not only a queer poet but also a Catholic girl from Boston, and these alternating identities are the key to who she has become and also what she can get away with. The narrator of *The Flamethrowers* has the same tendency, insisting on her obscure past in Nevada, knowing it makes her both interesting and, on a deeper level, able to disavow the excesses of the art world. I can relate, as I moved to L.A. clinging to the purity of my provincialism, proud of my innocence of freeways and IKEA.

I also relate, though, to Eileen and the narrator of *The Flamethrowers* as they try to assert themselves as artists, despite all appearances. I worked long days at a restaurant in West L.A., where, more than ever before, I felt the disconnect between the myth of myself and my daily reality. "I'm a writer," I insisted to my coworkers, and at the time I took their blank reactions as misunderstanding. They understood me. They all had ambitions, too. Now I see this as the ultimate in a kind of classist and racist pretension. I thought they all belonged there, but I didn't. We want our humble, middle-of-nowhere histories to illustrate how unprepared we were for the city and how much we needed from it. We want them to differentiate our Hello to All That from everyone else's in their trials and triumphs. But of course everyone has a history: a story about themselves that says, "Don't blame me."

2.

I bought two paperback copies of *The Flamethrowers* in the summer of 2014 at Skylight Books in Los Feliz: one for me and one for my boyfriend, C. Then I went outside to find that one of my car's tires had deflated on a jagged curb on Vermont Avenue. My trunk was too forbiddingly stuffed with junk to access my spare tire, so AAA towed me to a tire yard on Fountain that was overrun with playing children, where I bought a random used tire for probably too much. My friends had been buzzing about *The Flamethrowers* for months. I didn't know it would mark the emergence of a journey both forward and back in time for me: a way to articulate the connections between the stories that preoccupied me. In a way, I started writing this book that day with the flat tire. I had been working on it before then, but I thought I was writing "about the noir." That day was when I slowly began to realize that my book was maybe not about the noir but about those forces of which the noir was a symptom, not about dead white girls but the more troubling mystery of living ones.

I knew I wanted to write about *The Flamethrowers* immediately. I saw in it an invitation to draw together some of my favorite books: Kushner was constantly compared to

Joan Didion. She was writing about the same art moment that produced Eileen Myles, whom I was obsessed with. It was like a supplement to one of my favorite Janet Malcolm essays, "A Girl of the Zeitgeist," about *Artforum* magazine, in which she documents the dying away of the conceptual art moment for the splashy, maximalist painting of the 1980s. The more I read, the more it all fit. I found a Myles essay about land artist Robert Smithson's *The Collected Writings*. Smithson, who created the famous *Spiral Jetty* on the Great Salt Lake, is Reno's favorite artist, and Myles also loves him. "Reading Smithson today I get a second glimpse at the New York I stepped into in the '70s," she writes. I mulled over this project constantly but barely put a word on paper about it. Nearly three years later, here I finally am. These books were such a part of my intellectual identity that to write about them would require uncomfortably reassessing them, and myself, too. I didn't want to question narratives about brainy, sad white women growing up or breaking down as they earned their cruel sentimental educations, because they assured me I wouldn't have to work on myself: the world would work on me.

Malcolm's "A Girl of the Zeitgeist" takes the form of a humorous eighty-five-page tour of artists' and art critics' New York lofts, as Malcolm travels around the city to interview them. Many of *Artforum*'s 1970s art critics were academics, who wrote articles as hard and dense as gemstones. The old guard of art critics were concerned that *Artforum* had become commercial with its hip new critics like the poet Rene

Ricard at a time when the price of art was skyrocketing. These 1970s critics were against pop art and the collapsing of high and low culture. "We felt that we had to make a distinction between Mickey Mouse and Henry James," one tells Malcolm, specifically blaming Susan Sontag for the trend of apostasy against high culture.

They believed that an art magazine should not have advertising and that artists should not care about money. As I read these conversations now, they feel like remnants of an America that was less shamefaced when it came to the calcified truth of class. The academic art critics were well-bred, Harvard-educated, and immune to money worries; thus they found the commercial distasteful. In their minds, it seems like their priestly class, freed from dependency on droning daily obligations and entertainments, is better able than workers to understand the anti-capitalist imperatives of Marx. Malcolm describes one of these critic's opulent loft with its "curved black sofa, mirror-topped coffee table, abstract and Oriental art, and fur-covered bed" as looking "more like a Park Avenue co-op than like a downtown living space," before the critic launches into a tirade about how bourgeois the art world has become.

In fact, "A Girl of the Zeitgeist" documents a theme that repeats in Myles's work and *The Flamethrowers*: the morning-after feeling that suffuses all art scenes, as discontented gate-keepers insist that the generation before you got there were the authentic artists and revolutionaries, and those in the scene now can hope only to drink from their dregs. Smithson died two years before the narrator of *The Flamethrowers* got to

New York. Eileen studies at the feet of the New York School poets, ten years after their 1960s heyday, still in the elegiac twilight of the death of Frank O'Hara. She and Ricard were friends, and they were both part of a new New York School, who, like their forebears including O'Hara, James Schuyler, and John Ashbery, frequently made money by writing about art. The 1970s academics despised how writers like Myles and Ricard applied the disarming intimacy of the poetry of the New York School to a new unbuttoned art moment. I see more and more that every avant-garde finds ways of looking not forward, but back, trying to strip away present encumbrances to return to a radically simpler version of beauty: from the Surrealists' belief in dreams disrupting industrial society to the seventies critics' desire to return to a time before the reign of Mickey Mouse.

The "girl" of Malcolm's title is Ingrid Sischy, who in 1979, at the age of twenty-seven, took over as editor in chief at *Artforum*. Sischy was an outsider, with experience in publishing art books but no training in art history, who brought to the magazine good instincts for provocative cover art, a desire for interesting, gestural writing, and extraordinary patience when dealing with artists and critics. Malcolm depicts her as the opposite of the 1970s art critics, innocent of ideological prejudice and possessing a very un-elitist obsession with ethics and fairness. Malcolm compares her relationship with Sischy with the frustration one feels toward the upright and optimistic heroines of Henry James: those "moments when the thread of sympathetic attention snaps and we fretfully wonder why these girls have always to be so ridiculously fine."

Rereading Malcolm, I did a double take at this passage. It had become almost eerie how often the literature of the nineteenth century, and particularly Henry James, was invoked to discuss the real and fictional inhabitants of the mid-century New York art scene. As much proof as I had that avant-gardes were backward-looking, I hadn't previously thought they looked back so far. In *The Importance of Being Iceland*, Myles sees the roots of radicalism and her artistic itinerancy in the nineteenth century, pointing out that the nineteenth was the century of Karl Marx, who invented the working class "like he's our Santa and we're the elves." In *The New York Times* review of *The Flamethrowers*, Cristina García writes that the book's narrator "is a modern Henry James heroine—a rough-riding Daisy Miller, say—who wanders far from home and submits to what turns out to be a very unsentimental education at the hands of reputed sophisticates."

The foremost of these reputed sophisticates is Sandro Valera, an older, well-established artist whose work consists of large, austere aluminum boxes. The narrator and Sandro fall in love, and he initiates her into his social world, immediately giving her access to a more glamourous New York than she could imagine from her dingy studio apartment on Mulberry Street. Sandro is the scion of Moto Valera, an enormous Italian motorcycle and tire manufacturer, and the narrator rides motorcycles, even riding a Moto Valera in college in Reno. In this coincidence lies her Jamesian date with destiny. She is obsessed with documenting the land speed trials at the Bonneville Salt Flats in Utah by entering them herself, hoping to create an art piece that melds the hick motorcycle culture of her upbringing and her conceptual interest in landscape, erosion, and duration.

To her own surprise, once at Bonneville, she sets a new female land speed record. She gets the opportunity to tour Italy with the Valera team, but first she must spend two weeks with Sandro's mother at the Valera family villa above Lake Como. The signora and Sandro's brother, Roberto, fear violence at the hands of the anarchists and unionists who are leading a workers' revolution in Italy. The tension of this dread is multiplied by the mute presence of the villa's servants, who lurk, almost invisible, at the corners of life in the villa. It turns out at least one of their servants really is planning to turn on the Valeras: they were marked people, just as they suspected. The narrator's problem is she doesn't know where her allegiance lies. She has ascended, a part of the class whom the servants wait on, but she relates to their invisibility, feeling distinctly unseen and unheard. Even after she has left the villa and joined ranks with the anarchists, she still holds herself apart: their invisibility is societal; hers is emotional, existential. Like I did with my coworkers at the restaurant, she makes the mistake of thinking her frustration is special.

As in any Gothic story, there is a genteel household in Western Europe paying for its plundering, a beautiful surface that cannot conceal its depths of moral ugliness, a brave new future that must pay for its barbaric past. As if to hammer home the backwardness of the decaying aristocracy, the narrator's final break with the Valeras comes when she finds Sandro kissing his cousin. But the narrator is just as corrupt, even if her failing is of a different kind. Her personal journey dwarfs the politics of the Valeras and the anarchists; those conflicts serve only as set pieces to illustrate inner conflicts. This is why she can infiltrate both worlds, so American, an emotional mercenary.

True to genre, my sentimental education also pivoted on a date with destiny. Having reached the age of twenty-five without achieving either of the milestones I associated with legitimacy—a real boyfriend or a real job—I was convinced that my time had passed, and I would never get either. In late April of my first year in California, my grandmother turned ninety. She had a potent matriarchal power: her little studio apartment was like her lair, cluttered with books, eldritch religious art, chocolate, and cookies. She never left except to go downstairs for meals, and she sat in her armchair with newspapers stuffed around her, along with holy cards and tokens in little pouches like a witch's hoard, watching *Murphy Brown* on DVD. On her birthday I talked to her about my woes and she told me that she would be saying Hail Marys for me. (This was her modification to the rosary that eliminated the boringly male Our Father and the dead weight of the Glory Be.) That night I got a call from an arts high school two hours east of L.A. officially offering me a job as their poet in residence, a real academic appointment. The night was glowing from a rare L.A. thunderstorm. While I was at dinner, I got a message on a dating app from my soon-to-be first boyfriend, C, asking if the storm had made the sky strange where I was, cloudy but bright.

For our first date he invited me to a barbecue at his house. "We're supposed to meet in a public place," I told him, reminding him of every cyber-safety tip I learned in the nineties. "I'm inviting a lot of people," he told me. "If you come to my house and there's no one out front, you can leave." There were a lot of people out front, including his childhood best friends and his brother. They were almost too welcoming. All of his friends were incredibly interested in my writing and my new job, and they had me read one of my poems out loud. C left me alone with them for so long that I wondered if he knew what a date was. But the timing was right: I longed for the normalcy of this kind of plan, buying a six-pack of beer and heading to someone's yard, petting dogs and meeting random neighbors and coworkers and friends of friends. I was so bored and lonely in L.A. that I would have rather gone to a barbecue than on a date.

That first date lasted for nearly twenty-four hours. I was immediately impressed that he could rent an entire house for himself and that he had maintained so many friendships for so long, attesting to how little anyone I had dated until then had had his shit together. He had poetry books on his shelves, which is easy to take as a sign. He later told me that he had ignored me on purpose at the barbecue, trying to gauge whether I could hold my own with his friends. He pointed to my success at this for our entire relationship as proof of my suitability for him. I wanted to tell him that this test of emotional strength was probably not only unkind but inaccurate. I was able to exist in his world as long as it felt like a game I was playing, one that reinforced the narrative of myself as able to fit in anywhere but belonging nowhere, privileged with a special separateness. It turns out this is the mental game many white women play in social (and societal) situations that they benefit from but are ambivalent about perpetuating. My trouble came when I realized that I was playing for keeps—or not playing at all but living my real, only life.

3.

Throughout her novels, Myles writes about the joys of playing everyday dress-up, wearing clothes that she finds at a party or in her mother's attic. She relishes recounting the fashion trends of her high school years, Madras shirts and "tennis sweaters, and penny loafers (with Madras in the slots) and boat shoes and low Keds and bold striped teeshirts." "I understood them in terms of uniforms because I went to Catholic schools," she says of her childhood love of clothes, "and also I understood them in terms of codes." When she describes the importance of performance in her work as an artist—first in poetry readings and later in writing plays and libretti—it feels like an extension of the same impulse. Performance and play are key to every cerebral work of queer theory of the past thirty years, but Myles makes it intuitive: performance is the mental games you play to entertain your friends and fight off existential boredom, which is why, for her, daily performance of identity and formal performances are not completely different. "Performance is spending," Myles writes in *Inferno*, but she later amends it to "recording," meaning that how we choose to act every moment we are awake is a way of paying attention.

She describes *acting* like a waitress when she is waiting tables, viewing it as a dress-up game or a performance project that reaffirms her true identity as a poet. The narrator of *The Flamethrowers* befriends a woman who tells her that she was an actress in Andy Warhol's Factory films, but she became a waitress as a piece of performance art. "I began to like it," she says, "the way it lent this air of tragedy to my so-called life." She tells the narrator about the diner's tacky decor, "my performance as a waitress, neon flashing into the room, making me feel as if I were living inside a film about a lonely woman who threw her life away to work in a diner. And I was that woman!" She also works as a prostitute, perhaps the only profession older than waitress. She makes the narrator think about how people negotiate double lives: How do you determine which one is your real life, the one whose truth arms you against the indignities of the second?

The narrator learns firsthand about the armor of identity: at the Salt Flats, she's not a racer, but an artist posing as one. After Sandro betrays her in Italy, she joins a group of young Italian anarchists in Rome. At first she films her experience with the anarchists, but even after her camera is broken during a demonstration, she is still convinced she is there as an artist and not a political actor. The mediating, passive eye of the camera helps hush the question of her complicity. We often think of artists' place in society as abrasive but neutral, there to witness and interpret, but not to participate. What a camera specifically does not capture is the person holding it, but we see the narrator as an accomplice in her ex-boyfriend's brother's murder clearly enough, as she aids his assassin's getaway through the Alps.

In both beliefs and bullshit, conceptualism easily blurs from artistic movement to political movement and back again. At a party filled with artists, critics, and gallerists, the narrator meets one of the leaders of a fictionalized anarchist group called the Motherfuckers who occupied the Lower East Side in the sixties, fighting cops and providing for the people. They took part in both real and symbolic acts of insurrection, committing fake assassinations with guns loaded with blanks. Clicking the kaleidoscope once, these "assassinations" could appear as a kind of performance art. The artist and the anarchist interact with the world through an abstracted scrim: for artists it is the concept, for the anarchist it is ideology, although these identities don't cleave in two that cleanly.

Describing her inspiration for *The Flamethrowers*, Rachel Kushner said that as she researched the New York art scene in the 1970s she was surprised to find "lots of guns, and lots of nude women." She collected picture after picture of male artists posing with guns, using that one object to broadcast the working-class, Wild West, tough-guy aesthetic they ascribed to, as they rejected the feminine gentility of previous generations of artists. Kushner writes about the driving force behind conceptual art:

> Art was now about acts not sellable; it was about gestures and bodies. It was freedom, a realm where a guy could shoot off his rifle. Ride his motorcycle over a dry lakebed. Put a bunch of stuff on the floor—dirt, for instance, or lumber. Drive a forklift into a museum, or a functional racecar.

In other words, seemingly radical art movements were based in part in the same retrograde idea of masculinity as the biker B movies that were popular at the exact same time.

But the nude women weren't just macho accessories. They were performance artists. Artists like Ana Mendieta, Yoko Ono, and Marina Abramovic used their own naked bodies to comment on the ways society used them, in graphic performances with titles like *Cut Piece* and *Rape Scene*. Feminist performance art was an ingenious exploration of the market value of the female body: although women's bodies are used to sell almost everything, through menial work and violence they are too often taken for cheap. Their work was an exploration of the performance required daily of all women. While men played at being outlaws with their guns, women played the parts given to them in order to survive.

I wasn't required to wear a school uniform as a child, but I sometimes wore my own version anyway, a navy blue jumper

I made my mother buy me at the Burlington Coat Factory. I played pretend in plain sight. When I was older, I imagined myself as a waitress in a movie to make food service tolerable. This was easier in Los Angeles where so many of the customers in this secret movie were played by actual movie stars.

Sometimes with C I felt like I was playing a part called "girlfriend," a role I'd imagined myself in my whole life. And as I emerged from the desert of my loneliness, the things we did together were like a glowing mirage. We tried every restaurant in L.A., including one where dessert was a flash-frozen orb of ice cream that looked like a dinosaur egg. We stayed in a boutique hotel on the beach in Venice. We took a train to Santa Barbara and went wine tasting. We traveled to New York City to go to a music festival. All of this was possible, of course, because C made several times more money than I did. I wasn't wrong that this life wasn't completely mine, because it was only mine as long as I was his.

In a way, the relationship was like a trap, but it wasn't the money that kept me there, as tempting as it is to paint myself like a Gothic heroine imprisoned in an evil lord's estate. I was more driven by the desire to appear to others as a girlfriend, which to me meant a normal woman. I loved C, but sometimes I worried that it wasn't the real me who loved him, but the girlfriend I was pretending to be. At the end of the summer, a few months after we started dating, I took a train up to Chico to see my aunt and uncle. C called me from a friend's wedding to drunkenly tell me for the first time that he loved me. He said that he was with all of his friends, so many people he loved, and he wished I were there, too. This indicated to him that he must love me. At the time I was dissatisfied by this reasoning, because I thought he was failing to honor the specialness of romantic love. I had longed for him to say that he loved me, but this didn't match my fantasy. Now I think the problem wasn't the lack of romance, but that his confession felt too real, addressed as it was not to a girlfriend but to me, myself.

I read most of Brendan Koerner's *The Skies Belong to Us: Love and Terror in the Golden Age of Hijacking* at LAX and on an airplane, so many passages are imprinted fittingly in my memory with images of glassy airport terminals and the navy Naugahyde of plane seats. Once I saw its cover— blaring red, white, and blue, with two early seventies faces, a black man and a white woman, staring out from it—I knew it would be another link in the chain I started with *The Flame-throwers*. I had an intuition about terrorism's relevance to the questions at hand, or maybe a belief that terrorism is relevant to everything.

The hijacking epidemic described in *The Skies Belong to Us* provides the perfect backdrop for the utter craziness and disillusionment of the era in which Eileen and Reno headed to New York, just after the shattered sixties. There were more than a hundred hijackings over the course of this bewildering fad, between 1961 and 1973. This crime appealed to the American (male) myth, weaponizing an emblem of modernity and freedom and promising ample institutional and media attention. It also engaged the American fantasy of getting something for nothing, be it a ransom or a trip to Cuba. Men of every age and ethnic group were susceptible to this fantasy, driven by a desire to reclaim their individual importance.

In fact it seems like the skyjacking wave encapsulated the marriage of optimism and nihilism that defines the American ego. Every hijacker believed that earning a stage from which to air his grievances would solve his personal problems and, if it did not, would cast him as a messianic figure, come to heal America's soul. At the very least, they would be choosing action against gray passivity. One hijacker explained his crime by saying, "Oh, yeah, something had to be done—and I did something, for better or worse." Hijacking was the last resort of people who would trade their freedom, even their lives, for a satisfying kind of self-expression, a chance to be the authors of their own stories, and there were many, many of those people in the United States.

These messianic fantasies were reinforced by the fact that a few hijackings succeeded by any measure. In 1969, an Italian immigrant hijacked planes all the way to Rome, where he was adored by the Italian public as both a teen idol and a folk hero. Then in 1972, a Mexican father of eight who had endured poverty and discrimination during his nineteen years living in the United States impulsively hijacked a plane and, instead of asking for ransom, requested that representatives of Los Angeles's Spanish-speaking media gather for a press conference. His desperate, maundering speech to journalists made him an icon of the burgeoning Chicano movement. "This is for save my sons and your sons, too. I am trying to save America, to save the whole world, because we are all crazy. We are mad," he told the pilot. Koerner writes that these hero hijackers "inadvertently tapped into a wellspring of rage." The hijacking phenomenon abounded with victims of the United States's sins of war and racism, wreaking havoc like vengeful ghosts. Many hijackers were disturbed veterans of the Vietnam War. In two separate cases, black residents of Detroit hijacked planes in order to protest the racism and corruption of the city's police department.

Roger Holder, the architect of the most successful hijacking of the era, embodied many of the grievances curdling inside his country. As a child, Holder saw his family experience vicious racism as the only black people in a small town in Oregon, then served several highly decorated (and severely traumatizing) tours in Vietnam. At the age of only nineteen, he was arrested for marijuana possession, court-martialed, and given the maximum sentence. He went AWOL and fled to San Diego, where he and his accomplice and girlfriend, a white California girl named Cathy Kerkow, were able to hijack planes all the way to Algeria to join a colony of exiled Black Panthers. After relations between the leftist regime in Algeria and the Black Panthers' "International Section" went south, Holder and Kerkow were able to follow the Panthers to France, where, thanks to an impassioned lawyer, they were not extradited to the United States. Despite his freedom and fame in Paris—Holder and Kerkow's social circle included Jean-Paul Sartre—Holder was racked by worsening mental illness and guilt over the twin daughters he had left in the United States. He experienced some of the struggles of black American expatriation that James Baldwin identified: that in order to achieve the kind of security one could not have in the United States, a black person must pay the price of complicity and self-hatred. As Baldwin wrote about Richard Wright, who lived in France for fifteen years,

> He was fond of referring to Paris as the "city of refuge"—which it certainly was, God knows, for the likes of us. But it was not a city of refuge for the French, still less for anyone belonging to France; and it would not have been a city of refuge for us if we did not have American passports.

Baldwin writes about the crisis of conscience when a person flees American oppression only to find out that they are more American than they previously thought.

Holder began regularly visiting the American embassy and begging to be allowed back into the United States, despite knowing that jail time awaited him there. He was eventually extradited back to the United States in 1986. Kerkow, on the other hand, adjusted eerily well to her glamourous life in Paris, wearing stylish, expensive clothes and speaking perfect French. She flirted with Sartre and was close friends with the actress Maria Schneider. Eventually her transformation was complete: in 1978, she said goodbye to Holder and slipped into Switzerland, most likely to buy a counterfeit passport, and she has never been heard from again. It is possible that she is still alive and incognito somewhere in Europe. The privilege afforded pretty white women allowed Kerkow freedom of movement, but what is more impressive about her disappearance is her determination and ruthlessness: she displayed a total lack of sentimentality about her past. Holder and Kerkow are almost too clean a case study in the differing relationships of black and white Americans toward their collective history.

The apotheosis of the white girl turned terrorist is Patty Hearst. The millionaire heiress of the Hearst publishing fortune was abducted from her apartment in Berkeley in 1974, just as Eileen and Reno were making their journeys to New York, and two years after Cathy Kerkow made her fateful plane trip. Her captors, left-wing terrorists called the Symbionese Liberation Army (SLA), held her blindfolded for fifty-seven days until she agreed to join their cause. After that, she participated in several bank robberies and, in the words of Joan Didion, "sprayed Crenshaw Boulevard in Los Angeles with a submachine gun."

Didion wrote about Hearst in 1982, on the publication of Hearst's memoir, *Every Secret Thing*. The book turned out to be misleadingly named, because even though Hearst includes tantalizing details about her sojourn with the SLA, like how to lace a bullet with cyanide, it was still unclear why she joined them, the extent that she believed in their ideology or was brainwashed, and how she could return so seamlessly to a relatively normal life when her captivity was over. In all, the question remained whether she was a perpetrator or a victim. Didion writes that public fascination cast Hearst's story as "a special kind of sentimental education, a public coming-of-age." But despite the public's desire for her to be like the ill-used heroine of a nineteenth-century novel, Hearst insisted on muddying the waters, writing in *Every Secret Thing* both fawning reminiscences of the Hearst family mansions and a description of how to make a pipe bomb. Her story illustrates that a sentimental education does less to destroy the innocence of its protagonist than reveal its falsehood.

"I know how power works," James Baldwin once said, "it has worked on me, and if I didn't know how power worked, I would be dead." Women know how power works, too, so often acting only out of a desire to protect our bodies from violence. "My thoughts at this time were focused on the single issue of survival," Hearst writes about the early days of her abduction. But the knot of victim and perpetrator doesn't always unravel so easily. White women wield power, too, particularly the power to enlist other people's protection and then leave them holding the bag, like every noir anti-heroine hiding secrets behind innocent eyes. After Reno abets Roberto's murder, she goes back to her job and friends in New York. Patty Hearst wrote *Every Secret Thing* "behind locked doors in a Spanish-style house equipped with the best electronic security system available." Cathy Kerkow was able to start a glamourous new life after committing the longest-range plane hijacking in history. These are representatives of a group of people who have gotten a little too good at survival.

Didion writes of Hearst as a daughter of the California pioneer ethic, for whom a connection to the past was a sentimental indulgence. "Patricia Campbell Hearst had cut her losses and headed west," she writes, "as her great-grandfather had before her." It seems more likely that she is the product of the United States's disordered relationship with its own history, which has allowed its people to live with massive moral contradictions from the moment of its founding. Hearst is America's sweetheart, reminding us that, as Baldwin put it, "this depthless alienation from oneself and one's people is, in sum, the American experience."

4.

Los Angeles for me was C. We talked about L.A. constantly, those conversations that so define the city's discourse that it's become a cliché:

"How did you get here?"

"We took Centinela."

"Should we Uber?"

"Can you pay the Uber there, and I'll pay the Uber back?"

"If you wake up early enough, you could take the 210."

"Oh, I *love* the 210."

He read Didion while we were together, and we tried to determine if the first essay in *Slouching Towards Bethlehem* took place in a part of San Bernardino County either of us were familiar with. Didion was all I wanted to be as a writer. I was obsessed with how her essays were literary but not academic, full of evidence but more about juxtaposition than justification. I see now that my mission inaugurated with *The Flamethrowers* was an attempt to discover who I could be as a writer without Didion as my guiding star. Her California was one I recognized, despite its being fifty years gone. I didn't realize then that it was partly because so many things had bent to her nostalgia: there were pictures of her leaning against that sports car everywhere, like there are pictures of Charles Bukowski in dive bars. C and I read *The Flame-throwers* together, too, part of an effort to have something to talk about other than driving and his dog.

It's easy for me to blame everything on Joan Didion. But if I weren't her acolyte, I probably wouldn't have been so contentedly miserable in Southern California. I was depressed and anxious most of the time C and I were together, a predictable recurrence of the mental illness I'd dealt with since I was thirteen. I had anxiety attacks at work, while driving, and when C and I were having sex. Often I would start crying and be unable to stop. It took me a long time to interpret these symptoms correctly. I thought I was "disorganized," had "writer's block," had migraines and allergies. I thought it was a symptom of the Los Angeles Didion described in her essays, a giant city sprawling with housing developments from the desert to the ocean, disconnected neighborhoods laced together by serpentine freeways, the alienation of which induces sensitive white ladies to nervous breakdowns. I was probably partaking in some of her glamourous desperation, too, the kind of privilege that allows one to suffer "migraines that can be triggered by her decorator's having pleated instead of gathered her new dining room curtains," as Barbara Grizzuti Harrison wrote in her epic anti-Didion rant in 1979, likening her to "a neurasthenic Cher." The fact that I was able to participate in everything that made Los Angeles exciting while still being unhappy felt very Didion indeed.

It seems simple now: I was starting a new job, splitting my time between the boarding school and L.A., a difficult two-hour drive I made several times a week, and I was uncertain about my relationship. None of these sources of stress had anything to do with abstractions about California's essential soul. I wish I had seen then that when Didion wrote about "Places of the Mind" she wasn't kidding: what she defined as California was a map of her own dread, but it didn't have to be mine.

Our cultural obsession with Didion and her generation of writers has only intensified in the two years since my L.A. era. As I write this in 2017, people seem to be constantly pointing to how thinkers of the twentieth century predicted the reactionary disaster of the Trump administration, from the Frankfurt School to John F. Kennedy. It's no coincidence that both a hugely popular documentary about James Baldwin, Raoul Peck's *I Am Not Your Negro*, and Didion's first book in six years, *South and West*, were released in spring 2017, and both were hailed as prophetic of our current political dilemma.

There is a feeling that the unfulfilled promise of the 1960s, when the hopeful uprising of the civil rights movement gave way to disillusionment with a series of traumatic assassinations and the quagmire of the Vietnam War, holds the key to our present moment. History cycled back as our beloved first black president and new protest movements could not stop a white nationalist billionaire from becoming the most powerful person in the world. In *I Am Not Your Negro*, Peck shows shot after shot of sneering white men and boys in the fifties and sixties, holding Confederate flags and signs that say WE WON'T GO TO SCHOOL WITH NEGROES. These images are eerily echoed in pictures of Trump rallies or of the college-aged white boys who have followed the far-right provocateur Milo Yiannopoulos on his speaking tour like he was a jam band, reveling in overt misogyny and racism rebranded as irreverence or "free speech." These far-right gatherings, organized and emboldened, grew to the open unity of the Ku Klux Klan, white supremacist groups, and racist Inter-net trolls in Charlottesville, Virginia, in August 2017, which resulted in a white supremacist murdering a protester with a car.

The problem of white femininity became more compli-cated after the Great White Woman Hope, Hillary Clinton, failed to break the "highest, hardest glass ceiling," and hundreds of thousands of liberal white women took to the streets the day after Donald Trump's inauguration in solidar-ity with their more marginalized neighbors, many of them for the first time. But another similarity in these pictures of angry mobs of white boys from 1957 and 2017 are the white girls lurking at their fringes. The famous photos of Char-lottesville are of white men with crew cuts and polo shirts marching with tiki torches, but there were white women there, too, supporting and in many ways protecting them.

We believe that staring hard at these ugly images of big-otry is necessary to inoculate ourselves against it, which is also why we seek the "prophets" of the previous generation, hoping not to repeat the mistakes of the past, as if there are ever any new mistakes. But I am not the first person to point out that it is easy for white people to enjoy delicious disgust at our misguided and hateful fellow citizens—it is both self-righteous and entertaining, knowing that *you* would never protest an abortion clinic or an integrated school, and if you did, you would at least spell *abomination* right. The long tradition of molding everyday bigots into clowns and monsters with the help of a pull quote and a telephoto lens continues unabated, despite our fear of repeating history. Simplifying these people is an act of charity, a way to sentimentalize them. This is why so many chroniclers of late sixties and early seventies America failed so completely, despite a manic obsession with the zeitgeist. Didion and other New Journalists depicted the politicians, protesters, criminals, and cultural icons of their era not as good guys and bad guys, but as the diverse avatars of historical absurdity. As Grizzuti Harrison wrote, Didion "is obliged to call attention—in a series of verbal snapshots, like a Diane Arbus of prose—only to the freaks of the 1960s."

The most telling example is the Black Panthers, whom both Didion and Tom Wolfe (especially in his satirical essay "Radical Chic: That Party at Lenny's") were drawn to because of the verbal novelty of revolutionary boilerplate language applied to the situation of the American ghetto. One of the pivots of "The White Album" is a visit to Huey Newton in prison, where he is playing the press like a fiddle, meanwhile saying very little about himself or his specific aims. "Tell us something about yourself, Huey, I mean about your life before the Panthers," one reporter asks. "Before the Black Panther Party," Newton replies, "my life was very similar to that of most black people in this country." Didion is obsessed with a story in which Newton was denied treatment at an emergency room because he did not have the proper insurance, thinking that it illustrated "a classic instance of an historical outsider confronting the established order at its most petty and impenetrable level." Her theory is destroyed when she learns that despite Newton's belligerence in the emergency room, he did in fact have the proper insurance. For Didion, Newton's status as "an historical outsider" collapses, confirming that the Black Panthers were just another group of actors in the political commedia dell'arte, all of whom are ridiculous and dishonest, and therefore easily and thankfully dismissed. Taken another way, this anecdote illustrates Didion's inability to parse the complexities of a black working class: that Newton could be initiated in some bourgeois institutions and still be oppressed by them.

As Baldwin points out in *No Name in the Street*, though Didion and Wolfe treat the Black Panthers as a novelty, the U.S. government took them seriously enough to act systematically "to wipe the Black Panthers from the face of the earth." It is difficult to properly stress the contrast between Baldwin's description of the Panthers' mission and New Journalists' condescension. Baldwin points out that the initial stated mission of the group was self-defense, teaching black neighborhoods to protect themselves, especially against a racist police force. Their visionary power was in precisely the details that Didion and Wolfe saw as spectacle. As Baldwin explains it,

The Black Panthers made themselves visible—made themselves targets, if you like—in order to hip the black community to the presence of a new force in its midst, a force working toward the health and liberation of the community. It was a force which set itself in opposition to that force which uses people as things and which grinds down men and women and children, not only in the ghetto, into an unrecognizable powder.

It is not hard to understand if for one moment you imagine that black people were telling the truth—that their revolutionary rhetoric was not an attempt to co-opt leftist machismo but was, in fact, a pointed call for a specific kind of justice. Baldwin discusses Huey Newton, too, but, unsurprisingly, lends him more thought and sympathy than Didion does. His descriptions of Newton are long and thoughtful, considering the contradiction of the clean-cut guerrilla who looks like "everyone's favorite baby-sitter."

The difference in perspective between Baldwin and these zeitgeist chasers is encapsulated in Baldwin's estimation of the difference between himself and another of their generation, Norman Mailer: "He still imagines that he has something to save, whereas I have never had anything to lose . . . The thing that most white people imagine that they can salvage from the storm of life is really, in sum, their innocence." There is something nostalgic in these bemused journalistic dispatches from the brave new world of the sixties, something of a desire to tame unruly social movements, to Make America Great

Again: "Somewhere between the Yolo Causeway and Vallejo," Didion writes in "The White Album," "it occurred to me that during the course of any given week I met too many people who spoke favorable about bombing power stations."

I remember realizing the danger in this weary stance toward history, shortly after seeing one of Woody Allen's crappy late-career movies with a friend back in Montana. It occurred to me that Didion (born 1934) and Allen (born 1935) took a similar self-centered view of the sixties and seventies counterculture: having been helpless children during the biggest disaster of the twentieth century, they tended to view despair not as political but existential. If you take this long view, it is easy to see all problems as equally pointless, allowing ethics to slip soothingly from your thoughts. Police brutality is a phenomenon similar to the popularity of the Doors in "The White Album"; Allen's heroes are equally preoccupied with memories of the Holocaust and losing their teenage girlfriends. But while Allen is easy to disavow, Didion's blind spots hurt in a childish way, like finding out my mom told a lie.

I should have guessed there was a problem with Didion's ethos when she questioned the use of narrative itself, asserting that life was more accurately portrayed as a series of disjointed vignettes, the clippings of discarded film edited from our stories. It's not that I think this is inherently wrong, and it wouldn't mean much if I did; fragmentation as an artistic technique is not going away. But when I read Didion's work from the 1960s and '70s, I wonder if "we tell ourselves stories in order to live" is maybe not stated in good faith, if this belief in the falsehood of narrative and the truth of fragmentation is another story we tell ourselves. The disconnectedness of her work is an ironic gesture, a way of illustrating her longing for the continuous and comforting narratives of the past. And it reflects romantic myths about California, about a place like a stage set, with no memory, no consistency, no true reality.

Nowhere is Didion's status as architect and propagator of false narratives of California clearer than when she is cunningly deflating sentimental myths about other places, foremost New York City. She of course wrote the most famous essay about getting tired of New York and leaving, "Goodbye to All That," but she is better and more brutal in her 1990 essay "Sentimental Journeys," about the Central Park jogger case, in which five black and Latino teenagers were convicted and imprisoned for a brutal rape they did not commit. There Didion explores how corruption and inequality are built into the structure of New York, and these essential qualities are written off or written over by platitudes about the city's "energy" and "contrasts." "The preferred narrative worked to veil actual conflict," she writes, "to cloud the extent to which the condition of being rich was predicated upon the continued neediness of a working class." This sounds pretty socialist coming from an erstwhile Goldwater Republican.

Her main critique is of the New York public mobilizing against the abstracted phantom of "crime," meanwhile ignoring "the essential criminality of the city." Crime stories are ubiquitous in our culture not only for their transgressive lure but for their power to reinforce a social order, providing "a sentimental reading of class differences and human suffering, a reading that promises both resolution and retribution . . . working to blur the edges of real and to a great extent insoluble problems." Particularly disturbing are the ways that white female victims become the mascots of campaigns against "crime," which can almost always be read as campaigns against a city's poor and nonwhite residents. In the Central Park jogger case, the crime's anonymous victim, a Wall Street executive who was gang-raped and beaten while jogging at night, was perversely idealized in the New York press, "wrenched, even as she hung between life and death . . . into New York's ideal sister, daughter, Bacharach bride." The traditional withholding of rape victims' names helped her fulfill every fantasy of "contrasts" between the city's best and brightest and its dark underbelly. It reinforced comforting notions of who was a girl—a twenty-eight-year-old investment banker, whose name was not spoken—and who was a man—a fifteen-year-old suspect who had not even been arraigned, whose name was spoken by the police and the press.

In the Central Park jogger case, black men and white women were cast not only as opposites but as natural enemies. In an op-ed for the *Daily News* after three defendants in the case were convicted by a female district attorney, Bob Herbert wrote, "They never could have thought of it as they raged through Central Park, tormenting and ruining people . . . And yet it happened. In the end, Yusef Salaam, Antron McCray and Raymond Santana were nailed by a woman." This is the vicious nature of envisioning a victim of a brutal crime as Lady Courage, as "New York rising above the dirt": the unwillingly canonized white girl becomes a new cudgel to punish those whom the city has always punished most. Didion writes passionately and convincingly against this weaponized white femininity in "Sentimental Journeys." But it was her, after all, for whom the murder of Sharon Tate, and not of Martin Luther King Jr., signaled the end of the sixties.

It is difficult for white women to take responsibility for our faces—looming from magazines, televisions, posters, blown up absurdly on buses and billboards—and the aims we've allowed them to be deployed for. In *The Flamethrowers*, the narrator works as a China girl, the white (not Chinese) women whose faces were cut into the beginnings of film leaders, "there for the lab technicians, who needed a human face to make color corrections among various shots, stocks, and lighting conditions." The narrator describes the obsessed crushes the lab technicians had on their favorite China girls, smiling, ordinary women whose regularity "was part of their appeal: real but unreachable women who left no sense of who they were." A split-second snippet at the beginning of a movie, most viewers would never see a China girl, and if they did, their gaze would not linger on her; the China girls were like subliminal messages, illustrating minutely codified standards of what was beautiful and what was normal. The China girl was the cheerful mascot of wholesomeness, and as such, she was the very face of white female complicity, gazing into the camera as defiant as Patty Hearst in her mug shot.

Didion wrote "Sentimental Journeys" twelve years before the five defendants in the Central Park jogger case were exonerated, when DNA evidence proved another man had committed the crime. In it, she is skeptical of the state's case against the five young men, noting inconsistencies in their confessions, and that the state "had none of the incontrovertible forensic evidence—no matching semen, no matching fingernail scrapings, no matching blood—commonly produced in this kind of case." Not knowing the extent of the travesty of justice the case represented, Didion sees it as a febrile shared narrative that produced hysteria in sympathizers on both sides, with the white leaders of the city indulging in their Mother Courage/anti-crime rhetoric, and black leaders inciting their community to paranoia.

But the case validated many of the theories that Didion quotes skeptically from the famous black newspaper the *New York Amsterdam News* of "a white conspiracy at the heart of [black] victimization." The defendants were, in fact, in the hands of "a criminal justice system which was . . . 'inherently and unabashedly racist,'" victims of "a 'legal lyching,'" of a case 'rigged from the very beginning' by the decision of 'the white press' that 'whoever was arrested and charged in this case . . . was guilty, pure and simple.'" Baldwin often describes the white ideal of innocence as a desire for an imagined past uncomplicated by the problem of race—for a simpler, whiter time. It may be that in "Sentimental Journeys," Didion, in her weary pragmatism, is unable to imagine the true face of innocence: not the China girl, but the scared black teenager giving a coerced confession. *I Am Not Your*

Negro tacitly asks who we are more likely to call a child: photos of white faces smirking below a sign that says GO BACK TO AFRICA NEGROES are juxtaposed with the faces of black lynching victims suspended above their broken necks.

Grizzuti Harrison's most searing criticisms of Didion are of her conservative politics, with her caricatures of sixties leftist movements illustrating her belief in "the futility of all human endeavor." When Grizzuti Harrison identifies Didion as residing "somewhere in Ayn Rand country," my notes say only "ouch." But the irony of Grizzuti Harrison claiming that Didion finds "any attempt at political analysis . . . perversely romantic" is that Didion spent most of the two decades after Grizzuti Harrison wrote this essay doing political analysis, writing about the politics of Central America and its diaspora, in *Salvador* and *Miami*, and covering American presidential politics for *The New York Review of Books*. Didion described her own foray into political reporting as Sisyphean and depressing, and it became an opportunity for her to once again rail against narrative, "the ways in which the political process did not reflect but increasingly proceeded from a series of fables about American experience." Grizzuti Harrison writes that Didion is notable in her unwillingness to connect the personal and the political, but it seems to me that politics is for Didion irremediably personal—it is so exhaustingly freighted with personalities that she can put no faith in it.

Didion exemplifies "the personal is political" as not only a rallying cry but a warning. Considering the crowded tradition of white female memoirists since Didion, I keep this warning in mind, given that telling a personal narrative, especially one anyone is interested in hearing, is a privilege in itself. In the half century since "the personal is political" was coined, many white women have interpreted it as "the personal is important" and taken it as a cue to appropriate public struggles to work out their individual grievances. Didion saw her private anxiety reflected in the chaotic state of California at the end of the sixties. The narrator of *The Flamethrowers* is stirred watching the women's groups in a demonstration in Italy, chanting, "You'll pay for everything!" "I took their rage and negotiated myself into its fabric," she says. "I fused my sadness over something private to the chorus of their public lament." And isn't this just an essay about my ex-boyfriend?

It is very difficult to avoid sentimental narratives in personal essays, given that we romanticize nothing so much as ourselves. This was what exhausted Didion about narrative, and I think many white women are trying to situate themselves in stories that they didn't invent and wouldn't have chosen. That does not erase responsibility for reproducing distorted myths about power, for obscuring the fact that our most common stories are our most political. The sentimental education is hardly an innocuous trope, particularly when white American women, from the heroines of Henry James to the narrator of *The Flamethrowers*, stand in for the innocence of their young country. Hellos to All That are not about genuine transformation, more often using a callow protagonist as a foil to illustrate the world's many cruelties. Such works do not properly illustrate a coming-of-age at all. This was a startling revelation about the literature of the sentimental education, but it still left me with a problem: How could I hope to grow up?

5.

Since Didion wrote her essay about leaving New York, the Goodbye to All That has become a cornerstone of the personal essay genre. Like the Hello to All That, the Goodbye to All That is built on myopic misconceptions about what makes a city unique—on sentimental, or false, narratives. Often their writers could not imagine living anywhere other than New York City or Los Angeles, setting the two cities up, ridiculously, as polar opposites. They are written by writers who are friends with all the other authors of the Goodbyes, thus creating a shared language that incorrectly defines a city as an elite living within it.

I like Didion's Goodbye, but my favorite is Mary H. K. Choi's mini-memoir *Oh, Never Mind*, even though it's roughly as traditional a Goodbye to All That as you could find. Choi describes how in her mid-thirties, after a decade in New York working as a journalist and editor, she moved to Los Angeles to work in TV. *Oh, Never Mind* is full of generalizations about New York and L.A. that are funny but relatively meaningless: "In New York, everyone thinks they're special; in Los Angeles, everyone feels entirely regular unless they're famous, which, as a percentage, is basically no one." She is self-conscious about the clichéd nature of her project.

"Letting go of New York was like breaking up with every boyfriend I'd ever had all at once," she writes. "And I know it's not new to want to leave." She even warns her reader against doing the very thing she's doing, advising that "the key to moving from New York to L.A. is to do it and not tell anyone," because the Goodbye to All That is so dramatic and such a bluff—so many Goodbye-ers eventually move back to New York, including Didion herself.

What is remarkable in *Oh, Never Mind* is how Choi veers from her meditation about New York City to plumb her distant past, evoking "the stankiest, fermentiest, bottom-of-the-barrel kimchi, and pickles that sizzle like pop rocks. A la recherché du temps perdu, or whatever." She writes about the confusion of growing up Korean in a multiethnic school in Hong Kong, where she didn't long to be white but to be English, and thought Asian kids who hung out with other Asian kids were pathetic because "they settled for what I'd perceived to be the Friend Starter Kit (Oriental flavor)." She writes about her adolescent eating disorder, with Karen Carpenter and Lifetime Movies making her bulimia a way of partaking in pop culture. She writes about her family's eventually moving to Texas and her roommate at UT, "a gorgeous socialite from Taiwan who spoke little English and dated guys who bought her clothes." It's almost as if leaving New York unleashed old versions of herself, alternative possibilities for who she could be given a change in geography.

This move, to pull the present away from the past in strips, speaks of the originating urge of autobiographical writing: to capture the way we experience time, which is not as a straight line but as layer after layer of experience that pile up inside the body. James Baldwin's writing is full of compulsive bursts of biography, and he often takes us all the way back. *No Name in the Street* begins with his mother holding a piece of black velvet cloth and saying, "That *is* a good idea." "We can guess how old I must have been," Baldwin writes, "from the fact that for years afterward I thought that an 'idea' was a piece of black velvet." The discursive essays that make up most of his nonfiction function almost as diaries, meditations on race, politics, and literature held together by reminiscences from his own life, often ones that don't completely resolve. *No Name in the Street* is peppered with the story of his former bodyguard's trial for a murder he didn't commit. In the book's epilogue, he says that he is still waiting to hear the outcome of the trial.

The book is also a story of reluctant Hellos to both New York and Los Angeles. In 1952, Baldwin returned to his hometown of New York from Paris, wanting to confront the America that had made him and to support the growing civil rights movement. His ambivalence toward New York draws a contrast with the soft-focus wistfulness of a typical Hello or Goodbye to All That: "No, I didn't love it," he writes, ". . . but I would have to survive it."

Throughout *No Name in the Street,* Baldwin documents his doomed project of writing a screenplay based on *The Autobiography of Malcolm X.* Though he doesn't write the end of that story either, he seems to see it coming. "What one can't survive is allowing others to make your errors for you, discarding your own vision, in which, at least, you believe," he writes. Like so many literary geniuses before him—F. Scott Fitzgerald, William Faulkner, Evelyn Waugh, and Nathanael West—who moved to Hollywood to sell out to the movie industry, he experienced a special kind of alienation in L.A., that exile of the swimming pool. "People have their environments: the Beverly Hills Hotel was not mine," he writes. "For no reason that I could easily name, its space, its opulence, its shapelessness depressed and frightened me." I have come to see the elements of biography in Baldwin's writing as Augustinian confessions: for you to understand where he is coming from, he will tell you where he came from.

This was an unsatisfying truth I acquired on my sentimental journey: that a life is *about* nothing except the reams of time that it is made of. This is one of those profundities that skirts the obvious, and the boring, too. Every book would be called *Being and Time*, but that title is taken. The writer is not only accounting for time but actually counting it: there's a reason poets talk about meter. In *Inferno*, Myles writes about her poems not as describing her life, but as the very atmosphere she's living in, an ever-present music enhancing her daily movements. "The room was the poem, the day I was in . . ." she writes. "These little things, whether I write them or not. That's the score." I love this sense that just as a poem winds its way down the page, you can use it as a meandering path through the world.

This way of thinking is common to conceptual art, which was an attempt to expand the definition of art to include all the objects and ideas the world could produce. Despite its as-

sociation with minimalism, conceptualism is a hungry movement, bleeding across all forms and playing with eternity,
with artworks as monumental as the Great Salt Lake. There
is a swaggering rejection of those constraints that are conces-
sions to the possible: in *The Flamethrowers*, one character
has an ongoing project to photograph every living person.
But some of this mania for comprehensiveness feels tinged
with wistfulness, too. I think of the hours-long sentimental
"diary films" of avant-garde filmmaker Jonas Mekas, intentionally amateurish, quiet clips from his everyday life among
downtown New York hipsters during the sixties and seventies, including his famous friends like John Lennon and Yoko
Ono. Mekas and his brother were imprisoned in a German
labor camp during World War II after escaping their native
Lithuania, and much of the sweetness of his films seems informed by this trauma. He has captured so many hours of
idyllic footage, you might begin to think it is a complete record of his life—it's an alternative life, a dramatic score, and
this one is for keeps.

The narrator of *The Flamethrowers* makes downtown
New York diary films, too, recording a row of limousines out
her window on Mulberry Street, waiting to take mafia men
home from their social club. Other than the performance
aspect of her run at the Bonneville Salt Flats, the only art
pieces we see her make are films, using the medium to capture stasis and speed. The obvious question when it comes
to conceptual art is how to record it and how much, and
whether that record is art unto itself. The narrator's hero,
Smithson, is famous for his audacious land art, but just as

compelling is his writing about his own work, his theories of "sites" and "non-sites" composed so clinically and then undone just as deliberately. "This little theory is tentative and could be abandoned at any time," he writes about non-sites. "Theories like things are also abandoned. That theories are eternal is doubtful. Vanished theories compose the strata of many forgotten books." It is amusing that the art critics Malcolm interviewed in "The Girl of the Zeitgeist" resented poet critics like Myles and Ricard, when those poets' work more closely approximates conceptual artists' own writing, which was gnomic and often crazy. As much as conceptualists wanted to reimagine art as "gestures and bodies," they encoded those gestures and bodies into a new landscape of words—theories, pronouncements, descriptions, suppositions, and yes, even feelings—which poets have been doing essentially forever.

I've always read and written to mark time, working my way through *The Flamethrowers* slowly, over many months in L.A. I stopped in the middle of the thirty-page-long party scene, so the night Kushner describes seemed to last not hours but weeks. Reading it over so long, I felt the narrator and her circumstances shift in what seemed like real time: the book is true to the bewildering way relationships and alliances and fortunes change, like the young artist who is begging for curators to look at his pieces with embarrassing desperation, and then, a few months later, is the hot newcomer in the art world, his pathetic earlier self completely forgotten. I read it during a hot, drought-ridden fall, when it was so dry outside that ants infested odd corners of C's house, getting into his freezer and attacking his ice cream sandwiches. Then in December, a monsoon that blew in from Hawaii flooded the freeways.

During that time I wrote a poem cycle based on James Schuyler's lovely poem "Song," his ode to the delicate moment of twilight, when "A cloud boy brings the evening paper: / *The Evening Sun*. It sets." I wrote a poem for every line in Schuyler's poem, taking it as my cue and, like the title poem of Schuyler's first book of poetry, "freely espousing." My poems are filled with dress-up games: "If I were a cartoon I would wear this every day," I write about "a halter dress that shines like root beer." In the same poem, I write that "in my '70s life / I am demure as a chicken strip." I was going for a Day-Glo, SoCal version of Schuyler's bucolics, describing how "Places in LA it is / true astroturf, / the Brady Bunch's / post-drought dream," but what resulted was more apocalyptic. I read all of my poems for my students and colleagues at my faculty reading that winter, and the next day felt so depressed and helpless that I cried myself hoarse when I couldn't find my keys. I abandoned my poetry project. The weather changing like a mood swing makes a nice backdrop, but I swear this isn't a sentimental narrative: my relationship was doomed.

If it isn't already obvious, most of my questions here are questions of conscience: How can I use the personal essay, instead of letting it use me? When I look at James Baldwin, one of the most deserving heroes of the form, I see a portrait of a true political artist, and all the difficulty that goes along with that position. *No Name in the Street* is the account of writing interrupted over and over again: he is called away from novels and screenplays by the assassinations of Malcolm X, Martin Luther King Jr., and Medgar Evers. He marches on Washington and fund-raises for the Black Panthers. And in the end, it was a book "much delayed by trials, assassinations, funerals, and despair." But he holds on to what art can do that politics can't: remind us that "the people are one mystery and that the person is another."

Unexpectedly, in the notes section of her book *On Immunity*, Eula Biss (author of another memorable Goodbye to All That, from her first collection, *Notes from No Man's Land*), writes a short meditation on the ambiguous place of the personal essayist:

> as a poet who writes in prose, or a prose writer informed by poetry, I have often found myself confronted with the question of belonging. The problem has not been finding a place where I belong . . . but of finding ways of insisting on belonging nowhere. To this end, I have tried to heed Alice Walker's lines "Be nobody's darling; / Be an outcast." The tradition of the personal essay is full of self-appointed outcasts. In that tradition, I am not a poet or the press, but an essayist, a citizen thinker.

The problem is that self-appointed outcasts like Didion, who looked at the most charismatic movements of her day with skepticism, have become everybody's darling. Grizzuti

Harrison says snidely of Didion that "many male critics find her adorable," but this isn't exactly Didion's fault. It's a case where celebrity has transformed an odd, prickly artist into a poster girl.

Being a darling is tempting, which is why I abided so long in an extended adolescence I didn't deserve and that didn't do me much good. C and I had a codependent relationship where I lolled around his house like an infant, and he resented me for it; then he bought everything for me, and I resented him for that. "You're saying he's the type who is into younger women?" the narrator of *The Flamethrowers* asks her friend about Sandro. "Sweetheart, that's all men," her friend replies. But C, who was four years older than me, hinted that he would rather date an older woman, saying when he turned thirty that women in their thirties would finally take him seriously. I was understandably offended. But I should have taken it as a clue that being a girl would not serve me forever.

If it ever served. In *Chelsea Girls*, a girl Eileen knows as a teenager goes on a beach trip with friends. She is lying by the pool passed out drunk when all the boys ejaculate on her face. "She was disgusting," the girl who invited her says. Another girl "had been gang raped one night and never seen again." Later in the book, Eileen recounts an experience she had at a beach house when she was eighteen. She was so drunk she remembers nothing except "the rhythm of many guys . . . I seem to remember all of them in there at once but that may have been a blur and then precisely Dave sitting down . . . saying you are disgusting, you are a slut." "Rape was the first sex I ever heard of," she says. Eileen's friend, the younger sister of one of her rapists, did nothing to protect her, saying that she thought Eileen liked it.

That is precisely the problem with white girlhood as a consolation prize from the patriarchy: it can offer adoration and protection, but it's every girl for herself. Women artists are wise to reject it, since our culture celebrates boy geniuses, but not many girl geniuses. One of the few is Taylor Swift, who has somehow stretched her public coming-of-age from her teens to her late twenties. I used to listen to her sad-sack songs on the bus in L.A. and actually cry. In the spring, when I was more than a little reluctant to move in with C, he bought us tickets to an end-of-summer Taylor Swift concert at the Staples Center that cost more than a thousand dollars. I begged him not to, but he did, and it was the perfect painful coda to our relationship.

At the end of my school year, when I knew I had to break up with C, I went to my parents' house in Nebraska for two weeks to think it over. I was a wreck with guilt and anxiety, having never had a conversation as consequential as a breakup. As I agonized to my mom, my younger brother told me, kindly, that my situation was simpler than it seemed. "You hear a lot of people say, 'Oh, yeah, I dated that person for a year when I lived in L.A. or wherever,'" he said. The only way to grow up is to realize that the little tragedies that shock and devastate you are actually universal and inevitable. You are not going to learn that by listening to Taylor Swift or reading Joan Didion, not that I intend to stop doing either. I wish this insight on people before they turn twenty-five, but it's better late than never.

I broke up with C on a Tuesday. At the end of the week I would go to Montana to lick my wounds for the summer before returning to the boarding school for work in the fall. For the rest of the week after the breakup, we had sweet, rueful dates, like going to the Americana in Glendale to eat dumplings and see an animated movie about anthropomorphic feelings. I could not have invented a more Los Angeles hipster destination for our very last date: a monthly invite-only farm-to-table pop-up in Santa Monica, several courses served on mismatched shabby chic wedding china. I accidentally wore the same thing I wore on our first date, because I wore it all the time, a ratty floral skirt I bought at Target when I was twenty. When we got there, groups of women were stepping from their Ubers in glittery cocktail attire. I had never exactly seen it before: how little I even looked like I belonged in C's world, how badly I had been playing my part the whole time. And I had never felt so acutely how little the perks of his Los Angeles were worth it.

In *Oh, Never Mind*, Choi writes that her last days in New York "were all about spending my not-very-much money on not being there. I'm all about that JOMO life: the joy of missing out." I have had a perverse version of JOMO my whole life, which is why I moved to Los Angeles and not New York, preferring to be stranded in a sun-bleached freeway labyrinth than to thrive in a literary hub where I could meet other people like me and most things are easily accessible by train. On our last date, I looked over the balcony at some Dumpsters and thought with bright relief about all I would be missing out on that summer. The day I left Los Angeles I steered my overloaded car north toward the desert, and I felt like myself, acting alone.

Acknowledgments

Versions of some of these essays have appeared elsewhere, many in different form. Thank you to my editors at the Awl, the Los Angeles Review of Books, the Toast, Broadly, *The Believer*, and This Recording for giving those pieces their first homes.

Thank you to my genius editor, Chloe Moffett, and the entire team at Morrow/HarperCollins. You made this book ten times better. Thank you to my acquiring editor, Marguerite Weisman, for making my dream come true—I will always be grateful. Thank you to my perfect agent, Monika Woods, who believed I was writing a book long before I did.

Thank you to the Department of Creative Writing at the University of Montana and the Montana MaFiA, without whose nepotism I would not be where I am today. Thank you to my writing professors at the University of Nebraska and the University of Montana, especially Rebecca Bednarz, Brian Blanchfield, Prageeta Sharma, Peter Richards, Kevin Canty, and Debra Magpie Earling.

Thank you to the Creative Writing department at Idyllwild Arts Academy and my dear colleagues Kim Henderson and Abbie Bosworth for giving me the time and support to write much of this book. Thank you to all my students at Idyllwild Arts Academy and the University of Memphis for your joy and brilliance.

To my many wonderful friends, colleagues, and mentors, especially Emily Jones, Zoey Farber, Emma Törzs, Virginia Zech, Andrew Martin, Breanne Reiss, Ed Skoog, and J. Robert Lennon, for your fellowship, encouragement, and advice, I thank you.

To my family, especially Tim Stuart, Fred Stuart, Willo Stuart, and Anderson Stuart, my love and thanks always. Thank you to Dan Hornsby for loving and believing in me, and for being my smartest and most helpful reader. To Mary Bolin, Bob Bolin, Tom Bolin, Charlie Bolin, and LaVon Crosby—I love you, and this book is for you.